RESEARCH ESSENTIALS
OF
ADMINISTRATIVE LAW

RESEARCH ESSENTIALS OF ADMINISTRATIVE LAW

H. B. Jacobini

Southern Illinois University
at Carbondale

Albert P. Melone

Southern Illinois University
at Carbondale

Carl Kalvelage

Dakota Northwestern University

Palisades Publishers

Pacific Palisades, California 90272-0744

To the memory of
Professor Orville Alexander,
departmental architect, master teacher,
wise man, and friend.

Library of Congress Catalog Card Number: 83–60926

International Standard Book Number: 0–913530–35–2

Front and back photographs: Federal Trade Commission Building
Washington, D.C.

Library of Congress Cataloging in Publication Data

Jacobini, H.B.
    Research essentials of administrative law.

    Bibliography: p.
    Includes index.
    1. Administrative law—United States—Legal research.
I. Melone, Albert P.   II. Kalvelage, Carl.   III. Title.
KF241.A35J32 1983   342.73'06'072   83–60926
ISBN 0–913530–35–2   347.3026072

Palisades Publishers
P.O. Box 744, Pacific Palisades, CA 90272–0744

Printed in the United States of America

Contents

PREFACE   ix
1   ADMINISTRATIVE LAW: AN OVERVIEW   1

How and Why Administrative Law Arises   1
Judicial Review   2
Agencies and Information   3
Rules: Quasi-Legislative Activities of Agencies   4
The Quasi-Judicial Role of Agencies   6
     Predictability   6
     Pretrial Process   7
     Hearings   7
     Evidence   7
     Bias and Interest   7
     Separation of Functions   8
     Exclusiveness of the Record   8
     Official Notice   8
     Burden of Proof   8
     Findings, Conclusions and Reasons   9
     Institutional Decisions   9
Informal Actions and Discretion   9

2   WHY AND HOW TO BRIEF A CASE   11

Elements of a Brief   13
Model Brief   15

3   RESEARCH IN ADMINISTRATIVE LAW   17

Introduction   17
Opinions of the United States Supreme Court   18
     United States Reports (U.S.)   19
     United States Supreme Court Reports—Lawyers' Edition (L.Ed.)   19
     Supreme Court Reporter (S.Ct.)   20

Lower Federal Court Reports   20
    Federal Cases (F.Cas.)   20
    Federal Reporter (F.)   21
    Federal Supplement (F.Supp.)   21
    Federal Rules Decisions (F.R.D.)   21
    American Law Reports (A.L.R.)   21
Federal Administrative Decisions   23
    Looseleaf Publications—Federal Decisions   23
State Court Reporters   29
    Looseleaf Services—State   33
Locating Administrative Rules and Regulations   33
    Federal Register (Fed. Reg.)   33
    Code of Federal Regulations (C.F.R.)   34
    State Registers and Administrative Codes   35
Legal Encyclopedias   35
    American Jurisprudence 2d (Am.Jur.2d)   38
    Corpus Juris Secundum (C.J.S.)   39
Codes   41
    United States Code (U.S.C.)   41
    United States Code Service (U.S.C.S.)   42
    United States Code Annotated (U.S.C.A.)   43
Digests   43
    American Digest System   44
      Key Number System   44
    Specialized Digests   46
      Federal Practice Digest, 2d   46
      U.S. Supreme Court Digest (West Publishing Company)   46
      U.S. Supreme Court Reports Digest: Lawyers' Edition   46
Citators   47
    Shepard's United States Citations: Cases   48
    Shepard's United States Administrative Citations   49
    Shepard's Acts and Cases by Popular Names   51
    Shepard's United States Citations: Statutes   51
    Shepard's Code of Federal Regulations Citations   52
Legal Periodicals   52
    Index to Legal Periodicals   53
      Subject and Author Index   54
      Table of Cases Commented Upon   54
      Table of Statutes Commented Upon   54
      Book Review Index   54
    Current Law Index   54
    Index to Foreign Legal Periodicals   55
    Index to Periodical Articles Related to Law   55
Law Dictionaries   55
Computer-Assisted Legal Research   56

Legal Research Exercises   56
    Exercise #1—Legal Encyclopedias   56
    Exercise #2—Legal Codes   57
    Exercise #3—Digests   57
    Exercise #4—Citators   57
    Exercise #5—Legal Periodicals   58
Answers for Legal Exercises   58

4   A SURVEY OF THE LITERATURE   **60**

Major Treatises, Texts, and Casebooks   60
Official Studies, Reports   62
Governmental Information Sources   64
Materials on State & Local Administrative Law   65
Some Historically Significant Works   66
The Regulatory Agencies   68
Administrative Discretion   70
The "Legislative" Courts   71
Military Justice   72
Comparative Administrative Law   72
International Administrative Law   75
Outline Series   76
Texts on Public Administration Containing Sections on Administrative
    Law   76

5   CITATIONS: FOOTNOTE AND BIBLIOGRAPHICAL ENTRIES   **79**

What to Footnote   79
    Quotations   79
    Facts   80
    Explanatory Remarks   80
Bibliography   80
Form   81
    Footnotes, General Rules   81
    Bibliography, General Rules   82
Books   82
Journal or Magazine Articles   85
Newspapers   86
Encyclopedias, Almanacs, and Other Reference Works Excluding Legal
    Materials   86
    Signed Articles   86
    Unsigned Articles   86
    Material from Manuscript Collections   87
    Radio and Television Programs   87
    Interviews   87
    Letters   87

Mimeographed or Other Nonprinted Reports   87
Pamphlets   87
Proceedings of a Meeting or Conference: Reproduced   88
Paper Read or Speech Delivered at a Meeting   88
Thesis or Dissertation   88
Government Documents   88
Congressional Documents   89
Bills   89
Debates   89
Reports   89
Hearings   89
Executive Documents   89
Executive Department   89
Presidential Papers   90
International Documents   90
International Organizations   90
Treaties   91
State and Local Documents   91
Legal Citations   92
U.S. Supreme Court   92
U.S. Supreme Court (Reporter's Name)   92
Federal Cases (F.Cas.)   92
Federal Reporter (F.)   93
Federal Supplement (F.Supp.)   93
Federal Rules Decision (F.R.D.)   93
American Law Reports (A.L.R.)   93
State Cases   93
Federal Register (Fed. Reg.)   93
Code of Federal Regulations (C.F.R.)   93
Legal Encyclopedias   93
Federal Statute   94
Federal Code   94
State Code   94
Federal Administrative Decisions—Official   94
Federal Administrative Decisions—Looseleaf Publications   94
Law Journal Article   95
U.S. Constitution   95
Second or Later References to Footnotes   95
Scientific Reference Form   96

6   GLOSSARY   99

7   SELECTED BIBLIOGRAPHY   123

INDEX   139

Preface

The needs of students of political science, particularly those in public administration, are the focal points of this work. It is designed to help in courses in administrative law and also in other public administration studies where law is a significant but not necessarily the central element.

This book contains a summary of the main themes in American administrative law; an introduction for students in how and why to brief a case; a legal glossary, particularly germane to administrative jurisprudence; a chapter on how to focus on pertinent research; an annotated survey of book literature; a chapter on footnote and bibliographic citations; and a selected bibliography. Some of this material is designed to press inquiries into comparative administrative law data beyond United States experience, but in all instances it is a supplement especially useful in helping students with pertinent research and is intended to save valuable class time for the instructor.

This volume is to be used in the development of research papers and in conjunction with other text and case materials.

The authors are aware of many intellectual and clerical debts which must go mostly unmentioned. Particularly helpful to us in this work have been staff members of the Law Library and of Morris Library at Southern Illinois University at Carbondale. Among those who should be especially noted are Professors Elizabeth Slusser Kelly, Elizabeth W. Matthews, E. Ann Puckett, Laurel Wendt, James W. Fox, Walter R. Stubbs, Carlos Marquez-Sterling and Charles Holliday. Many persons have helped with parts of the typing and checking references; in this connection Sandy Hickam, Peggy Melone, Carol Leach, and Cass Van Der Meer have carried considerable burdens, all of which is greatly appreciated.

In special areas of study we recall with warmth the help, insight, and guidance of former teachers. Professors Edwin Stene of the University of Kansas, Edward M. Goldberg of California State University, Los Angeles, and John R. Schmidhauser of the University of Southern California are gratefully noted in this connection.

Alan Scott and Derek Johnson of Palisades Publishers have been supportive and helpful with many details. Our families, too, have been patient burden bearers in their own right, and we acknowledge these debts with appreciation and affection.

H.B.J.
A.P.M.
C.K.

1

Administrative Law: An Overview

Administrative law, a branch of public law, consists of those norms establishing and governing public agencies and offices, the rules that such agencies themselves make, and the court rulings that circumscribe agencies and their rules. Much of the process is set forth in basic national and state procedural laws, usually known as the *Administrative Procedure Acts* (APA). For reasons of brevity, this chapter will center upon federal procedures, but the reader should realize that somewhat parallel state procedures operate as well.

This sketch will look at administrative law in six categories: (1) how and why it arises, (2) judicial review of agency actions, (3) administrative acquisition of data, (4) quasi-legislative activities, (5) quasi-judicial activities, and (6) informal administration and discretion.

HOW AND WHY ADMINISTRATIVE LAW ARISES

Whenever a government administrator is authorized to do anything, law-making potential exists. When he does take action and makes a decision, he has created a rule; when he decides a disputed view he has acted like a judge. These points should be self-evident, but what makes it all vital is that over the past two centuries, governments have relied increasingly upon these techniques in creating a great many agencies to carry out the innumerable activities of government. In this connection governments have created administrative agencies and offices for the express purpose of making rules and deciding disputes based in both instances on the expertness of the government agency and its officers. It is said that many of these activities are too technical for the legislature to legislate specifically and for the courts to adjudicate. These grants of authority and power are called delegation.

Traditionally delegation seemed to contradict the authority of separation of powers, and indeed in strict logic it does so. Nevertheless, it is believed necessary in order for modern governments to perform the many services which are demanded of them. The real question is not whether there is a delegation of legislative authority; rather, the issue is whether an unwarranted delegation of legislative authority exists.

Finally, it is imperative that government be fair, and the processes of administrative law represent an attempt to permit government to do what is demanded of it, and to create processes designed to keep it within the bounds of fairness, due process, and democratic legitimacy. Comparative administrative law treats of the processes used in other societies to achieve some of the same objectives. These processes are not always the same as those in our society, and it is instructive and useful to compare and contrast such procedures with our own. Sometimes such processes are usable in different polities, note, e.g., the increasing use of the ombudsman, which originated in Scandanavia, in American and other governments.

JUDICIAL REVIEW

As noted above, the courts may determine whether agencies and the executive generally are acting within the bounds of legality. This is known as judicial review. But if courts heard *all* of the potential legal problems in the administrative sphere, they would do nothing else. Nevertheless, for some students of administrative law, the circumstances of such review are the alpha and omega of the subject. For students of public administration, however, the role is less all encompassing, but no question exists that judicial review sketches the parameters. What are the main guidelines?

Are areas present in which the administration is immune from legal restraint? The answer is a qualified yes. In the first place, certain executive acts are such that the courts will not, or are not likely to, review them. This concept is known as *sovereign immunity*, and while it is not as extensive as it once was, it is not yet completely dead. Many military matters are included here, but there are others as well. It appears now that the president may not be made the subject of civil suits at all for his actions, and while he is not immune from criminal prosecution, he seems to be relatively free.

Second, government is often immune from liability for damages. This is known as freedom from *tort liability*. Accordingly, a person injured on a public job usually cannot sue the state unless it has given permission under the terms of a so-called "tort claims act." But this, too, as a facet of sovereign immunity, is much reduced in scope.

Third, it is not at all certain that one can get advice from a public authority and not find that the authority will renege on its word and seek to have the party held responsible for an act for which the agent or agency seemingly gave permission. In private law this is normally impermissible under the doctrine of *estoppel*. But *estoppel* is only sometimes applied against government, and often denied. The point is that governmental administration must not be too fettered to function. Some of it, e.g., denial of estoppel, seems grossly unfair, but nonetheless important.

A second broad area of judicial review has to do with the circumstances under which courts will limit jurisdiction for what may be called primarily judicial reasons. In this connection courts exercise restraint in regard to the expenditure of court time. As noted above, if they did not, the dockets would become hopelessly clogged. Accordingly, courts limit what they will review on the basis of its triviality, or its lack of legal character, and for other reasons, including political, as well.

Among the more important limitations upon the exercise of judicial power are those based on *exhaustion of remedies*, questions of *primary jurisdiction*, *ripeness*, and *standing*. These doctrines are separate, but seem to overlap as they all are used by the reviewing court to say that the time, circumstances, or condition of the issue requires that they not review the question—at least at this time. The first of these, exhaustion of remedies, demands that the review process be completed in the agency before court review. The second, primary jurisdiction, determines whether the court or the agency should hear the case first. The third, ripeness, is concerned with whether the issue is sufficiently "developed" for the court to review, more specifically whether it has become a true controversy, rather than hypothetical, and whether there is a "record" (i.e., a detailed written official account) sufficient for review. Finally, if a potential litigant or his interest (i.e., his stake in the issue) is too remote, the court is likely to refuse to act, holding that the plaintiff lacks "standing."

Congress often endows an agency with authority to make certain final determinations. When this happens, the agency is said to exercise *action committed to agency discretion by law*. There are areas such as social welfare and security, veterans' affairs and immigration in which the sheer number of cases is staggering. Accordingly, many issues end with the agency decision and never reach a court of law. When a court is asked to review a case of this sort, it normally may be expected to deny itself jurisdiction unless there is some overriding consideration, such as action in excess of granted powers, lack of procedural due process, constitutionality, or an absence of substantial evidentiary support in the agency decision. In short, certain sorts of judicial intervention are warranted only if an administrative decision is clearly arbitrary.

AGENCIES AND INFORMATION

Agencies need and in fact have the power to acquire data pertinent to their activities. Since government agencies are creatures of the legislature, and do in fact "legislate," their powers to investigate pertinent to their rule-making authority are very much like the powers of the legislature to obtain information. This activity, arbitrarily and capriciously employed or improperly misused and disclosed, represents a potential nightmare. Conversely, individuals involved in agency litigation must be able to procure information in defense of their arguments. Further, there is the public's need to know what government is doing. Finally, there are the rights of the individual in regard to the information the government possesses about him or her including reasonable privacy. These are the aspects of information and data to be noted here.

In acquiring information pertinent to their functions, agencies possess wide but not unlimited latitude. Physical inspection of property is often employed, usually but not always with the need of a warrant. Testimony can be compelled by requiring presentation of company records, by compelling testimony under grants of immunity and by requiring that certain records be kept. The courts impose some limitations, but they are not altogether the same as those which protect private individuals.

A second aspect of information concerns the rights and needs of individuals. A facet of this problem centers on the needs of the person who is involved in an agency case. Usually available to him is a limited right-of-subpoena, a paler version of the one involved in a regular court trial.

A third facet of concern is the matter of privacy and accuracy of information about a given person. Consequently, contemporary federal law requires considerable confidentiality of personal records, and allows the individual access to much of the information about him held by the government.

A fourth major area has to do with the public's right to know and is a matter of great current interest and concern. With some exceptions agencies are now generally required to function in the open. The terms of those requirements are spelled out in the federal Freedom of Information Act and in state sunshine acts. The federal law obliges agencies to publicize such matters as their acts, procedures, functions, final orders, rules, and staff manuals. State sunshine laws require that most meetings be open to the public. The pertinent federal requirements are also a part of the Administrative Procedure Act.

Not all executive functions are affected by these norms. Probably the most notable exception is *executive privilege*. Under this debatable principle the President can refuse to reveal information; but like most aspects of information procurement and dissemination, this is subject to judicial review.

In summary, it is fair to conclude that with limited exceptions, while government has wide latitude in data procurement, it must be open about it. Within this framework, individual privacy enjoys considerable protection.

RULES: QUASI-LEGISLATIVE ACTIVITIES OF AGENCIES

When government agencies promulgate regulations, they are legislating. Depending on the enacting process employed, these are known as *rules* or *orders*. Whatever the label, these regulations possess the force of law. Agency lawmaking takes three forms: *informal* rule-making, *formal* rule-making, and *hybrid* rule-making.

Informal rule-making is the most straightforward method of agency legislation. It is established in the Federal Administrative Procedure Act (1946) and many states have similar enactments. By this process the agency follows a four-step process. 1) The proposed rule is published in the *Federal Register*; 2) following notice, interested parties may influence the outcome; 3) considering these inputs, the agency formulates the rule and publishes it, to take effect usually in 30 days; 4) there is to be opportunity for interested parties to urge the change, acceptance, modification or negation of the rule. This process is sometimes called *legislative* rule-making, and is widely acclaimed as the best means of agency legislation because it is relatively unambiguous, inexpensive, and straightforward.

Subsets within the informal rule-making category are two other somewhat comparable forms called *procedural* and *interpretative* rule-making. Both are normally of secondary importance. The first of these outlines the agency's internal and personnel processes; the second is a device by which agencies indicate their understanding of the meaning and scope of their basic charter laws. Interpretative rules may create legal problems, especially where the chartering legislation is itself ambiguous. Under such circumstances some courts have tended to substitute their judgments for the agencies'.

Formal rule-making is the second major form of legislating by agencies. It is less straightforward, more convoluted than the informal method, and complicated by its judicial form. In effect it is a kind of quasi-judicial legislating and employs essentially the same processes as the quasi-judicial function per se, which is presented later in this chapter. This formal rule-making method of agency legislating is set forth in section 554 of the Administrative Procedure Act (APA) and is also referred to as "rule-making on the record." The end products, however, ordinarily are called "orders" rather than "rules." The procedure entails a hearing held by an examiner or administrative law judge with a detailed pattern of submission of "evidence," requirements of proof, and the development of a "record," that is, a formal written account comparable to a court record. Since Congress and state legislatures often mandate such procedures, this "formal" process is widely employed, and it is often very costly. The notorious peanut butter case lasted over nine years, filled a record of more than 7700 pages and established that peanut butter must be 90 percent rather than 87 percent derived from peanuts. At that point it went into the courts and finally ended two and a half years later in effect by upholding the final agency order.[1] A better way is needed.

A third rule-making process may be called *hybrid rule-making*. In these instances Congress or state legislatures, and sometimes the courts themselves, have required agencies to follow processes which are more detailed than informal rule-making, but less complex than the formal variety. For example, Congress has sometimes required—in addition to the APA mandated processes found in section 553 and as a part of the specific rule-making process to be used by a particular

---

1. For an account of all this see Robert W. Hamilton, ''Rule-Making on the Record by the Food and Drug Administration'' 50 *Texas Law Review* 1132, 1142–45; Corn Products Co. v. Department of Health, Education and Welfare, Food and Drug Administration, 427 F.2d 511 (3d cir); and certioiari denied by Supreme Ct. Derby Foods, Inc. U. FDA, 400 U.S. 957 (1970).

agency—that certain specific consultations be carried out; that an advisory committee be created and consulted; or that an oral hearing be employed. These are less demanding than the requirements for rule-making on the record as set forth in section 554 of the APA but they are more burdensome than 553 alone.

Related complications are found also in some other processes sometimes required. Consequently a state legislature may use a special committee to oversee the making or modifying of agency rules. Typifying direct legislative overview is the section in the Illinois APA which provides for a "joint committee on administrative rules." While that committee cannot itself negate a rule, it can delay its taking effect and can seek nullification by the state legislative resolution. Its leverage is enormous.

The foregoing sketch outlines the main rule- and order-making forms employed by agencies. It deserves repeating that critics and serious students of these processes are generally agreed that the informal system of rule-making is, for the reasons noted above, superior. Accordingly, where there is opportunity to choose methods, the informal process is preferred.

THE QUASI-JUDICIAL ROLE OF AGENCIES

Whether performing "rule-making on the record" or more patently adjudicating, the process is the same. Agencies in their adjudicatory capacities serve as courts. The processes they employ are significantly circumscribed by laws, rulings, and appellate court decisions. All of this represents a specialized aspect of constitutional law, but even more important to the science of public administration, it represents a collection of procedures most of which reach beyond the mere administrative adjudicating process per se. There are some eleven facets which are important when considering the quasi-judicial functions of agencies. They are: (1) predictability, (2) the pretrial process, (3) hearings, (4) evidence, (5) bias and interest, (6) separation of functions, (7) exclusiveness of the record and ex parte communications, (8) official notice, (9) burden of proof, (10) findings, reasons, and opinions, and (11) institutional decisions.

Predictability

Predictability is a background consideration. It simply acknowledges that a norm once established should be consistently applied in the future. Predictability is far from an absolute principle or requirement, but it is the administrative law version of *stare decisis* (stand by past decisions).

It is useful to realize that the best way to achieve consistency is to institute a rule and then follow it. When adjudication is used, it may impose a new rule via the adjudication process itself, entailing in that instance a measure of retroactivity.

Pretrial Process

Like courts, agencies must use some pretrial activities. These represent attempts to resolve problems prior to actual trial and to clarify the issues. "Pleadings" and "discovery" are the principal descriptive terms. The former pertains to an exchange of charges or positions; the latter is a mutual disclosure of facts and documents; either may result in a "summary judgment," i.e., settlement in advance of trial, or in mediation.

Hearings

If the issues are not so resolved, they lead into the trial process which centers upon the hearing. The hearing is the key to proper procedure and must be conducted in a fashion so that the parties are free to respond to each other. Consequently, it must be open; counsel should be available when needed; parties with sufficient interest should have access; and the hearing should be held by a suitable examiner or administrative law judge.

Evidence

An administrative hearing, like a judicial trial, is concerned with proof. In order to establish proof the parties present evidence which must be at a particular level of certainty and adequacy. It must be open to rebuttal, and circumscribed with at least minimal rules and requirements. The so-called "rules of evidence" were developed for jury trials and are usually considered more important in that context than where the decision is made by a judge or an administrative law judge. These rules often seem to center upon the exclusion of certain kinds of evidence, especially so-called "hearsay evidence," but it seems less important, at least in the administrative setting, to exclude hearsay than to put the emphasis on responsible and intelligent evaluation of evidence. Unlike criminal cases which require "evidence beyond a reasonable doubt," and civil cases in which "a preponderance of evidence" is needed, administrative law cases are usually dependent on "substantial" or "clear and convincing" evidence. The federal APA expresses it thus: "on consideration of the whole record . . . and supported by and in accordance with reliable, probative, and substantial evidence." All this means that the courts may look askance at an administrative ruling that does not rely on at least some evidence appropriate to a jury trial, but beyond that they lean toward evidence sufficient to convince reasonable persons and/or evidence of the sort which reasonable persons use in making practical decisions.

Bias and Interest

A key to the fairness of an administrative trial is the absence of bias and interest by the hearing officer. Together these mean that the facts about the case not be prejudged, that the judge not be prejudiced against one of the parties, and that the judge not be in a position to achieve any personal gain by his decision. It does not mean that the judge must entirely lack a substantive point of view.

Separation of Functions

An important development over the years is the emphasis on separation of functions, often ignored in earlier times. Accordingly, the personnel of an agency who investigate and administer are usually not the same people who carry out the judging function. The APA states that administrative law judges "may not perform duties inconsistent with their duties and responsibilities as hearing examiners." But note the problem below when so-called "institutional decisions" are made.

Exclusiveness of the Record

Except for some truisms subsumed under the concept of "notice," which will be described later, a decision by an administrative tribunal is supposed to be based upon material dealt with openly and included in the written account of the hearing process. This is known as exclusiveness of the record. Thus, it is inappropriate for the officer who decides a case to have private discussions with one attorney or party, to receive gifts from a party, or to hold certain contacts with agency administrators. Pressuring influences by a member of Congress seems in principle to be no exception to this, yet it appears that it is sometimes a problem—and at least to an extent—it seems not altogether preventable. All of this proscribed activity would be off the record and is labeled *ex parte communications*.

Official Notice

In contradiction to the exclusiveness of the record principle, courts and agencies do in fact admit information not in the record. For agencies this is called "official notice," for courts "judicial notice." It consists largely of self evident truths or facts, undisputed and easily verifiable; e.g., U.S. Interstate 70 runs generally east and west. For agencies, official notice may also utilize some aspects of the agency's expertise. The Illinois APA specifies for example that "Notice may be taken of matters of which the circuit courts of this state may take judicial notice. In addition, notice may be taken of generally recognized technical or scientific facts within the agency's special knowledge." Such "notice" is inevitable, but fairness requires opportunity for rebuttal, which in fact does not always exist.

Burden of Proof

Another procedural aspect, known as burden of proof, requires simply that someone must have the primary responsibility to establish the proof. In administrative law this is usually whoever proposes a new rule or order, and in common practice this is the agency. But where official notice has been taken, burden of proof shifts to the party questioning that notice.

Findings, Conclusions, and Reasons

When the decision itself is made, there must be a full explanation, referred to as findings, conclusions, and reasons. "Findings" deal with facts, while "reasons" concern law, policy and discretion. The APA requires "a statement of findings and conclusions, and the reasons and basis therefore, on all material issues of fact, law, or discretion. . . ." Courts have required this as essential for review, and it is necessary also if a party desires a rehearing. Like research documentation, a statement of findings and reasons helps the agency to recognize its own powers, limitations and requirements.

Institutional Decisions

It remains to be noted that while an agency's action is heard usually by an administrative law judge, his decision is only a formal recommendation to the agency. It appears that these recommendations normally are accepted, but some serve only as the basis for the decision at a higher echelon in the agency which in fact need not follow the recommendation. This sort of determination, in which the agency as a whole makes a decision and/or where the ultimate ruling is made by an officer high in the agency, is known as an institutional decision. While the requirements of a fair hearing are presumed to be as applicable here (i.e., to the officer who ultimately makes the ruling) as to an administrative law judge, there are some annoying differences. It is said that the institutional decision draws on the "superiority of group work," but it is easy to see that inappropriate off-the-record factors may intrude. Courts have said that "the one who decides must hear," but this lacks its apparent meaning because the courts have defined hearing as being in "the artistic sense of requiring certain procedural minima to insure an informed judgment." The deciding officer can consult within the agency but not with prosecutors and investigators, and he must be informed enough about the record to render a proper decision. Reviewing courts will satisfy themselves that such requirements are met.

What this all means is that agencies, when they act as courts, must operate within certain procedural limits.

INFORMAL ACTIONS AND DISCRETION

A contemporary emphasis in administrative law centers upon the fact that definitive actions by executive departments—not only those of the regulatory agencies—have an official and legal quality about them. Indeed these aspects constitute the bulk of decisionmaking, and perhaps 95 percent of the decisions are made informally—even casually—on all levels of contemporary government. While some of this is circumscribed by restraints, much decisionmaking entails a great measure of discretion and is in fact subject to little review. Examples often noted are most decisions of the policeman on the beat; the prosecutor's decision to prosecute; innumerable IRS and social security determinations; and the bulk of matters in the areas of foreign affairs, defense, and immigration. There are many more.

Some of this is unlikely to change, but much discretion seems superfluous, even dysfunctional. Although the court decisions are not altogether clear, some reforms are urged and seem to represent directions for the future. A probability in federal law is that "courts should require administrative officers to articulate the standards and principles that govern their discretionary decisions." This seems to be gaining ground in the states as well.

The public administrator should be prepared to account for his actions and, whenever possible, those actions should be structured under a framework of standards, rules, and reasonable explanations. Other mechanisms include a system of checks by higher officials of subordinates' actions, use of ombudsmen, emphasizing precedent, use of advisory opinions and opinions of attorneys general and requirements of legislative oversight.

The thrust of practical administrative law for the future is to accommodate the need for increased administrative action to the equal need of a democratic society that these actions be fair. Prior standards, consistency, opportunity for citizen complaint; ample use of hearings, and openness, combined with curbs on irresponsible administrative behavior, seem indicated. Government must be able to act and to possess discretion but it must be suitable discretion, not profligate.

2

Why And How To
Brief A Case

Being asked to brief cases is a common requirement in administrative law courses. Some students will have briefed constitutional law cases. For many, however, a course in administrative law will be their first and perhaps last academic exposure to great quantities of legal material that includes judicial or quasi-judicial opinions. But any initial disadvantage may be overcome in weeks by the actual experience of briefing cases. At any rate this is consistent with the authors' experience over the years in a number of public law courses. Any student of reasonable ability and sufficient motivation can master the task of briefing cases.

Let us first define the task. Contrary to what some students have assumed, briefing a case for course discussion is vastly different from preparing a legal brief. We are not referring to a formal oral or written argument presented by legal counsel to a court of law. Rather, within the context of an administrative law course, briefing a case means reducing the written opinion of a court to its most essential elements. Typically, full opinions of reported cases are many printed pages long. Editors of instructional casebooks reduce these full opinions to the parts of the cases they believe are most relevant. Although editors occasionally will summarize the facts of a case, they usually adhere to the original wording of the opinion. They delete those words, sentences, paragraphs, or sections they regard as not instructive. Occasionally an instructor will send students to the library to read and brief a case from the full reported opinion of a court or administrative agency. Most often, however, instructors will ask students to brief cases that have been edited and placed in a course-required casebook. The result is that much of the analysis of the case is already completed by the editor and the student need only further reduce the opinion to its bare bones.

Briefing cases serves five purposes. First, it is practically impossible to recall, on the basis of one or two readings, a large number of cases discussed in a typical administrative law course. Besides the number of cases involved, administrative law cases tend to be complicated and turn on detailed facts and legal determinations. The information can be implanted in the student mind by writing down the essential elements of each case.

Second, if students read and brief the assigned cases as the course progresses, they can then review those cases before an examination, making the connections required. To attempt to read, comprehend, and remember law materials for the first time the night before a scheduled examination is to invite academic disaster.

Third, the very act of reading and briefing cases provides a dominant method for understanding how the law develops and changes over time. The growth of the law is traced through a series of cases; the earlier cases serve as the precedent and foundation for present cases. The student gains an appreciation for the historical method of the common law by observing the intimate relationship between the facts and decisions of past and current cases. In most law schools, the case-method approach, as it is known, is exalted as the best way to train attorneys. This contention has been hotly debated as tending to blind students to extra-legal material relevant to policy-making. Social scientists are generally alert to this problem.

It is desirable to employ some aspects of the case-method approach for at least three reasons. (A) It is necessary to know what the courts have said. They make policy and it is vital to know precisely what the policy is, if public administrators are to act consistent with legal mandates. (B) Students of politics should understand the workings of the legal mind and this can best be accomplished by studying lawyers and judges on their own turf and in their own terms. To be sure, the terms are often narrow and confining. But unlike law students and working attorneys, a clear understanding of the cases is not the end of analysis; for political scientists it is just the beginning. Political scientists must learn what the law is and then explain why the decisions were made the way they were, how the cases reflect values in and out of courtrooms, the public policy consequences of adjudication, and the social significance of the decisions. (C) Public administrators should understand how judges and quasi-judicial officials think about their policymaking roles. Armed with this understanding, professional bureaucrats are better able to predict judicial reactions to their decisions and actions. Knowledge of the workings of the judicial mind in this age of judicial intrusion into the administrative process is an indispensable requisite for effective administration.

A fourth justification for briefing cases is that it provides student and teacher with a common point of departure for discussion. Possessing a common text, one in which real people are in actual conflict, a class is in the position to discuss not only what might appear to be mundane legal issues, but also the often dramatic implications of decisions for government and society. Because such discussions must touch upon almost all aspects of social science and the humanities, students come to appreciate the interdisciplinary nature of the subject matter. The synthesis of ideas can and often does occur in such a charged intellectual setting.

The fifth and final justification for briefing cases is the lasting value of disciplined thinking. The experience of rigorous reading and writing will endure long after the cases become dim recollections. The careful and thoughtful process necessary for writing briefs introduces an appreciation for critical thinking and prepares one for future challenges. Because it helps to train the mind to be alert and requires careful written analysis of real life problems, the act of briefing cases is a worthwhile enterprise; this alone is sufficient justification, given the goals of liberal arts education.

ELEMENTS OF A BRIEF

What follows is a listing and discussion of the basic elements of a brief. A model brief is also provided. It should be noted that there is no accepted standard for brief writing. Instructors often have their own recommendations for the desired form. Yet our presentation is fairly consistent with most recommendations. It must be emphasized that a brief should be brief. Moreover, writers should make a serious effort to put the brief in their own words.

I. *Name or Title of Case*. This should appear at the top of the page and centered.

II. *Legal Citation*. The citation of a case is the location in published reports where full reported opinions of the case may be found. Usually a single citation will suffice; e.g., 379 S.W.2d 450 (Ky. 1964). If parallel citations are available it is wise to include them as well. Knowledge of case locations will ease the library search if at some later date it becomes desirable to read the full reported opinion.

III. *Statement of Facts*. The facts include the circumstances of the dispute giving rise to the lawsuit. But for purposes of a brief, only those facts treated by the author of the opinion as relevant, and those facts specifically treated as irrelevant, should be included in the written brief. Usually, but not always, the facts appear at the beginning of the written opinion. It is sometimes necessary to search the majority—and on occasion the concurring and dissenting opinions—for a complete statement of the facts. This statement should include the history of the case and how it came to be decided by the present court.

Because an object of the brief is to condense the opinion of the court, writers of briefs should make every effort to put the facts in their words. This is not always possible, but it should be attempted when practical. Use identifying quotation marks when phrases are lifted from any part of the opinion.

IV. *Statement of Issues*. An issue is a precise statement of a legal question facing a court for resolution. It is not uncommon for an administrative law case to have more than one issue. Sometimes the court must answer affirmatively one issue before it can or needs to answer following issues. It should also be noted that editors of instructional casebooks will often delete sections of a case which are deemed unimportant. Students should be aware of this fact since often one may read about a case in one context and subsequently is surprised that the case stands for much more in another.

Authors of majority opinions will often place the statement of issues in a clearly identifiable place within the text of the opinion—usually immediately after the recitation of the facts of the case. However, like the facts, the issues too are sometimes scattered through the entire written opinion. It is therefore important to analyze the full text before noting the issues.

Two rules should be followed when stating the issues: (1) the statement of the issue(s) should be put in the form of a question; and (2) the issues should be stated in an exact and specific manner. A case always involves answering a specific concrete legal question. American courts—federal courts in particular—avoid hypothetical or general issues—the statement of issues should reflect the actual case or controversy requirement.

A proper statement of the issues is very important because it reflects an understanding of the facts, conditions the legal decision, and places in perspective the reasoning of the court. Careful wording of the issues often produces long conditional interrogative sentences. And this is all right. Given the nature of the facts, statutes, or constitutional provisions, such sentences are necessary because they admit of no useful alternative. In any event, write the issues so they can be understood. At times copying the issues as stated by the court is the best format. However, whenever possible, put the issues in one's own words, making sure to keep those vital words or phrases of the opinion that are indispensable to understanding.

V. *Decision and Action.* For the decision simply provide a yes or no answer to each issue stated in Part IV of the brief. No explanation is required at this point. You may be asked to state the "holding" or "ruling" in a case. In such an instance recast the issue statement, depending upon the yes or no response, into a declaratory statement.

The *action* of the court will usually appear at the end of court's written opinion. It directs that something should be done; e.g., case reversed, or reversed and remanded, or affirmed, injunction granted, and other possibilities. Write down the court's *action* immediately following the *decision*.

VI. *Reasoning of the Court.* The reasons for the court's decision is the heart of the opinion. The reasoning contains the court's attempt to justify its decision in the case. But not everything written may be relevant for the purposes of the brief. Only that part of the reasoning which is directly supportive of the decision is appropriate for inclusion in the brief. There is often argument which is not directly related to the issues and decision in the case. This verbiage is usually referred to as obiter dicta, or simply obiter, or dicta, or dictum. It is, so to speak, excess intellectual baggage—argument unnecessary for the court to come logically to its decision in the case.

Given the basic objectives of a brief, one must read the court's opinion carefully, separating those reasons which are essential for the decision from those that are not. The key to separating the wheat from the chaff is the statement of the issues. Only those arguments necessary for supporting the answers to the issues should be part of the brief. Obviously this task requires careful reading and analysis. At first, novice brief writers will encounter difficulties. With experience this artful task becomes easier.

On the first line of this section of the brief note the author of the court's opinion; e.g., Per Clay. It is also wise to number the reasoning consistent with each statement of the issues. This permits quick eye movement among the issues, decision, and reasoning.

VII. *Concurring Opinion(s)*. A concurring opinion agrees with the result of the majority decision but disagrees with the reasons ("The right deed for the wrong reason," as one poet has put it.) Note the writer of such an opinion and briefly state his reason for the disagreement.

VIII. *Dissenting Opinion(s)*. A dissenting opinion exists when there is disagreement with the court's judgment in terms of both the result and the reasoning. Note the person writing such an opinion and the reason for disagreement.

IX. *Voting Coalition*. Few instructional casebooks provide complete information on the voting distribution of reported cases. However, if the information is available note the judges or justices voting together. This information is of interest when examining the politics of decisionmaking.

X. *Summary of Legal Principle(s)*. Briefly summarize the legal principles for which the case might stand. This is a good method for pulling the elements of the case together and is a valuable study aid when preparing for examinations. Also note how the case might differ from previously studied cases on the same topic.

XI. *Free Space*. Sometimes during class discussion the flaws in one's own brief become apparent. Leaving room at the end of the brief for revised comments is an efficient way to note needed changes. Classroom comments on the case might also be placed in this space. A separate notebook may be used for such purposes.

MODEL BRIEF

I. American Beauty Homes Corporation v. Planning and Zoning Commission.
II. 379 S.W. 2d 450 (Ky. 1964).
III. *Facts*: The appellant, an owner of a land parcel in a Kentucky county, petitioned that county for a change in the zoning classification from a one family residential to a commercial district. The county zoning commission denied the request whereupon the appellant brought suit in a circuit court which heard the case *de novo* (the entire case reheard as to both matters of fact and law). The appellant was required to present its case first and the trial court found in favor of the zoning commission. American Beauty Homes Corporation then appealed directly to the Kentucky Court of Appeals.
IV. *Issues*: (1) Did the trial court err in improperly imposing the burden of proof upon the appellant and not upon the commission?

(2) Is the constitutional principle of separation of powers violated when a trial court conducts a *de novo* proceeding?

(3) If a trial court lacks constitutional authority to review cases *de novo*, does it have any legitimate role to play vis-a-vis administrative agencies?

(4) Were the actions of the zoning commission arbitrary?
V. *Decision and Action*: (1) Yes; (2) Yes; (3) Yes; (4) No. Affirmed (i.e., it upheld the circuit court).

VI. *Reasoning*: Per Clay (Commissioner of Appeals). (1) The trial court did not shift the burden of proof upon the appellant. Rather it simply changed the order of the proof by requiring the appellant to present its case first; the burden remained with the zoning commission. (2) By granting to the courts the power to review *de novo* actions of zoning commissions the state legislature imposed upon the courts nonjudicial duties. But the legislature may not reduce or enlarge the scope of the judicial function. The statute permitting *de novo* proceedings makes the detailed administrative process a "mockery" because the steps taken there are simply repeated by the trial court. Thus, the trial *de novo* procedure is unconstitutional and null and void. (3) Three grounds exist for judicial review of administrative decisions. They are: (a) "action in excess of granted powers," (b) "lack of procedural due process," and (c) "lack of substantial evidentiary support." These three areas of judicial concern may be summarized under the concept of arbitrariness. The fundamental question in each case is: "Was the administrative decision arbitrary?" (4) The only possible claim of arbitrariness must be in respect to whether substantial evidence was available to support the zoning commission's decision. Yet clearly such evidence is present. The appellant was able to show only that the zoning change requested would be no more than a convenience to it and to the neighboring property owners in the immediate area. On the other hand, the zoning commission was able to demonstrate that the original residential zoning was in the best public interest.

VII. *Concurring Opinion*: None.

VIII. *Dissenting Opinion*: None.

IX. *Voting Coalitions*: Not Applicable.

X. *Summary*: When an administrative agency is promulgating a zoning plan it is carrying out a legislative policy granted to it and its function is nonjudicial. The legislature may not delegate administrative powers to a court. The scope of judicial review is limited to questions of arbitrariness.

XI. *Free Space*: (Leave approximately one-third of a page for comments.)

3

Research In Administrative Law

The focus of this chapter is on the basic research tools needed to get at administrative legal materials. Students must come to grips with the basic legal research materials common to all public law subjects as well as those unique sources available when researching a strictly administrative law topic. Although not particularly difficult to use, administrative law sources require identification and some attention to details. Our purpose is to introduce national, state, and local materials as well as a few comparative avenues of approach. The materials included here represent a substantial quantity but no attempt is made to exhaust the subject. Nevertheless, knowledge of the materials contained in this chapter will aid greatly in the successful completion of the most demanding administrative law assignments.

INTRODUCTION

Experience teaches that once political science and public administration students plunge into legal materials, they typically find the work informative and enjoyable. The common initial fear of legal reference works is easily overcome by actually working with the materials and can be mastered by anyone with reasonable intelligence. We have endeavored to present these materials with a minimum of assumptions about educational background and as free from unnecessary legal jargon as possible.

Most colleges and universities will possess much of the general legal research material discussed. Those institutions with law schools will naturally provide the richest experience. For some researchers inadequate holdings will be encountered. But even this may not constitute an insurmountable obstacle. Many community libraries possess adequate law collections, and many state governments provide law libraries for public use. Depending upon one's location, administrative law materials tend to be slightly more difficult to obtain than the more general legal library sources and references. This is true because administrative law tends to be of a more specialized nature and many libraries without request for such items choose to allocate funds for the acquisition of more popular items. In any event, always investigate the alternatives. If one library does not have what you want, try another.

The reported opinions of law courts are the primary source for all legal research in common law countries. Student textbooks usually contain edited versions of the written opinions contained in court reporter systems. Without such opinions it would be impossible to cite cases as precedent, and the principle of *stare decisis*—stand by past decisions—could have little meaning. The sources for administrative law opinions are varied. They may be found in general court reporter systems, which are discussed immediately below, to the more specialized administrative law reporters including federal agency reports, state reports, and international agency reports outlined later in this chapter.

OPINIONS OF THE UNITED STATES SUPREME COURT

Many landmark administrative law opinions have been handed down by the United States Supreme Court. Indeed, a large proportion of cases discussed in the classroom involve Supreme Court decisionmaking. Many court opinions, including those of the nation's highest court, are published by both government printing and private publishing firms. This is why it is possible to encounter more than one citation to the same case, e.g., *Securities and Exchange Commission* v. *Chenery Corporation*, 318 U.S. 80, 63 S.Ct. 454, 87 L.Ed. 626 (1943). Citations found in a series are often referred to as parallel citations. Three citations for the same opinion are presented for the *Chenery* case. The first, 318 U.S. 80, refers to the official government publication, *United States Reports* (U.S.). The number preceding the letters U.S. (318) refers to the volume, while the number following U.S. (80) indicates the first page in volume 318 of *United States Reports* at which *Securities and Exchange Commission* v. *Chenery Corporation* appears. The second citation (63 S.Ct. 454) refers to the place in the *Supreme Court Reporter* where the *Chenery* case may also be located, i.e., volume 63 beginning on page 454. The remaining citation is to volume 87 of the *United States Supreme Court Reports—Lawyers' Edition* (L.Ed.) beginning on page 626. *The Lawyers' Edition* (L.Ed.), like the *Supreme Court Reporter* (S.Ct.), is a private company publication. The year in which the opinion is rendered is placed in parentheses following the references to the various reporters, in our example (1943). One often finds parallel citations to the identical case because researchers often have access to only one of the court reports.

All three of the court reports have a common feature. Each presents the written opinions of the Supreme Court. They differ in the special features each possesses. The *United States Reports* (U.S.) is an official report and should always be cited first. The *Lawyers' Edition* (L.Ed.) and the *Supreme Court Reporter*

(S.Ct.) are unofficial publications of private firms and need not be cited if the official citation is presented.

United States Reports (U.S.)

The first ninety volumes of this official report contain the names of the court reporter. From 1790 to 1874 the court reporter's name is on each volume and is cited, giving the reporter's name, e.g., *Calder* v. *Bull*, 3 U.S. (3 Dall.) 386 (1798). Commencing in 1875 the *United States Reports* are designated by volume number, starting with number 91 and the letters "U.S." *United States Reports* (U.S.) contains the official opinions of the United States Supreme Court, summaries of facts, syllabuses, and indexes. Syllabuses, sometimes referred to as headnotes, are brief summaries of the important aspects of cases and contain references to the pages of the written opinions carrying significant legal points.

A "slip opinion" is issued a short time after a Supreme Court decision is handed down. This opinion is its initial issue and most libraries that obtain the bound volumes of *U.S. Reports* will also receive and make the slip opinions available. And they, at the end of the Court's term, are replaced with permanent bound volumes.

United States Supreme Court Reports—Lawyers' Edition (L.Ed.)

A publication of the Lawyers Co-operative Publishing Company and the Bancroft-Whitney Company, *United States Supreme Court Reports* is an outstanding private publication. It contains all high court opinions, starting with Volume 1, and has accompanying tables of parallel references to the official *United States Reports*. In addition to a faithful reproduction of the opinions as they appear in the official reports, the *Lawyers' Edition* has a number of features valuable to students of public administration and practicing attorneys. Editors prepare their own summaries of each case with headnotes (syllabuses). The appendix of each volume includes abbreviated versions of the briefs of counsel and annotations discussing important legal developments reported in the official cases. For example, the case of *Schweiker* v. *Wilson*, 67 L.Ed. 2d 186 (1981) gave rise to an annotation on the constitutional validity of a nongender-based classification such as age, legitimacy, mental health, and marital status with respect to benefit eligibility under the Social Security Act. This ten-page essay located at the back of the volume is a complete and up-to-date treatment of the topic. As the need arises, it will be supplemented with a pocket insert at the back of the bound volume. In short, the headnotes and annotations are most helpful to anyone interested in understanding legal developments including those in administrative law.

The *Lawyers' Edition* is kept current with twice monthly publications of *Advance Sheets* when the Supreme Court is in session. The *Advance Sheets* contain the most recent decisions of the Supreme Court with various research aids furnished by the editors. Together with other Lawyers Co-operative publications, the *Lawyers' Edition* is an outstanding research tool.

Supreme Court Reporter (S.Ct.)

This unofficial law reporter possesses many of the same features as the *Lawyers' Edition*. It is issued by the West Publishing Company and its headnotes and other references correlate with other West law publications. It is also supplemented with semi-monthly advance sheets when the Supreme Court is in session. The major disadvantage of the *Supreme Court Reporter* is that it begins with Supreme Court cases since 1882. Nevertheless, as part of West's National Reporter System the *Supreme Court Reporter* is very useful.

LOWER FEDERAL COURT REPORTS

Although U.S. Supreme Court decisions are of great importance, the lower federal courts handle a large amount of the administrative law litigation. United States district courts and the courts of appeal deal with many issues which, for one reason or another, are never decided by the highest court. These decisions may have far reaching policy implications and should not be ignored. Few if any research projects would be complete without a careful study of decisions issued by the lower federal courts. Students must be aware of developments there and certainly be familiar with the reporting system.

Federal Cases (F.Cas.)

Until 1880 opinions of the federal district courts and the circuit courts of appeal were scattered through a variety of law reports. The situation was remedied when in that year the West Publishing Company of St. Paul, Minnesota reprinted all the previously reported federal cases in *Federal Cases*. Cases are usually reported in chronological order. However, the 31-volume *Federal Cases* is an exception. Aided by a volume combining index and digest, cases are ordered alphabetically by name of case.[1] The following is a sample citation: *Pritchard* v. *Georgetown*, 19 F. Cas. 1348 (C.C.D.C. 1819) (No. 11,437). This unusual citation form signifies that the *Pritchard* case may be found in volume 19 of *Federal Cases* beginning on page 1348. The opinion was handed down by the Circuit Court of the District of Columbia in the year 1819. The last element of the citation contains the sequential number assigned by the publisher to the case, i.e., 11,437.

---

1. J. Myron Jacobstein and Roy M. Mersky, *Fundamentals of Legal Research*, 2d ed. (Mineola, N.Y.: The Foundation Press, Inc., 1981), p. 36.

Federal Reporter (F.)

Also published by the West Publishing Company, the *Federal Reporter* contains cases delivered since 1880. Presently in its second series (F.2d), the *Federal Reporter* makes available opinions from: (a) the United States District Courts (1880–1932); (b) the U.S. Circuit Courts for the period 1880–1912, and U.S. Court of Appeals (1891–present); and (c) a number of specialized courts students of administrative law may find useful including: the Commerce Court of the U.S. (1911–1913), the U.S. Court of Custom and Patent Appeals (1929–present), the U.S. Emergency Court of Appeals (1942–1961), the Temporary Emergency Court of Appeals (1972–present), and the United States Court of Claims (1929–1932, 1960–present). Opinions rendered by the U.S. Court of Appeals should be cited as follows: *National Labor Relations Board* v. *Rich's Precision Foundry, Inc.*, 667 F.2d 613 (7th Cir. 1981). Note that the particular circuit court is specified.

Federal Supplement (F. Supp.)

The *Federal Supplement*, also a West publication, reports decisions of: (a) the U.S. District Courts (1932-present); (b) the U.S. Court of Claims (1932–1960); (c) the Court of International Trade, earlier named the U.S. Customs Court (1956–present). The following is a sample citation for a U.S. District Court: *Diamond* v. *Federal Bureau of Investigation*, 532 F. Supp. 216 (S.D. N.Y. 1981). Note that the particular district court is named in the citation, i.e., the U.S. District Court for the Southern District of New York.

Federal Rules Decisions (F.R.D.)

This, too, is a West publication. Unlike the other federal reporters discussed, *Federal Rules Decisions* is not likely to receive much attention. The reported opinions involve U.S. District Court cases interpreting the Federal Rules of Civil and Criminal Procedure which are not reported in the *Federal Supplement*. The following is a sample citation: *Johnson* v. *North Carolina State Highway Patrol*, 91 F.R.D. 406 (1980).

American Law Reports (A.L.R.)

The *American Law Reports* does not fit neatly into the category of a court reporter. This is so because *A.L.R.* does more than report cases, and in four of its five series it reports both federal and state appellate cases. The editors of this Lawyers Co-operative and Bancroft-Whitney publication choose those appellate cases they feel are of general legal significance—cases that illustrate important legal developments. Following the judicial opinion, an impartial scholarly treatment of the law relevant to the particular case is provided. Each annotation is a detailed treatise on the specific legal topic. The annotation discusses in great detail the inception, development, and contemporary applicability of the law relating to the reported judicial opinions. Each annotation is updated by supplementing services, which should always be consulted.

There are currently five *A.L.R.* series. *A.L.R. 1st* covers the period 1919 to 1948 and contains 175 volumes. *A.L.R. 2d* includes cases and annotations for the period 1948 to 1965 and appears in 100 volumes. *A.L.R. 3rd* annotates federal and state law materials for the years 1965 to 1980 and since 1969 contains only state law topics. From 1969 to the present date *A.L.R. Fed.* reports only federal law topics. Lastly, *A.L.R. 4th* began publication in 1980 and it, too, is a contemporary series. A variety of handy subject and case indexes accompany each set.[2]

The author or title of annotations should not be referenced when citing any *American Law Reports* series. A sample citation is: Annot., 58 A.L.R. Fed. 834 (1980). Researchers investigating current issues in administrative law will find *American Law Reports Federal (A.L.R. Fed.)* informative. Immediately below are seven of the 50 or more annotations indexed under the ''Administrative Law'' topic between 1969 and 1981.

1. ''Energy Policy and Conservation Act: construction and application of § 382(b) of Energy Policy and Conservation Act of 1975 (42 USCS § 6362(b)), requiring certain federal agencies to include, in any major regulatory action, statement of probable impact of such action on energy efficiency and conservation,'' 48 ALR Fed 895 (1980).

2. ''Necessity for federal agency to order de novo hearing where presiding employee at agency adjudication under Administrative Procedure Act (5 USCS § 554(d)) must be replaced during hearing,'' 51 ALR Fed 470 (1981).

3. ''Extraordinary circumstances: what are 'extraordinary circumstances' of 29 USCS § 660(a) which permit judicial review of matters not raised before Occupational Safety and Health Review Commission,'' 52 ALR Fed 867 (1981).

4. ''Davis-Bacon Act: legal issues relating to wage rate determinations by Secretary of Labor under § 1 of Davis-Bacon Act (40 USCS § 276a),'' 53 ALR Fed 272 (1981).

5. ''Notice: compliance with provision of Administrative Procedure Act, 5 USCS § 553(d), providing that, with certain exceptions, required publication of a substantive rule must be made at least 30 days before its effective date,'' 54 ALR Fed 553 (1981).

6. ''Freedom of Information Act exemption (5 USCS § 552(b)(5)) for inter-agency and intra-agency memorandums or letters as applicable to communications to or from attorneys for the government,'' 54 ALR Fed 280 (1981).

---

2. *The Living Law: A Guide to Legal Research Through the Pages of A Modern System* (The Lawyers Co-operative Publishing Company, Bancroft-Whitney Company, 1982), p. 18.

7. "Privacy Act amendment of records: what action may be required of federal agency in suit by individual to have records amended, pursuant to § 3 of the Privacy Act of 1974 (5 USCS § 552 (g)(1)(A))," 55 ALR Fed 338 (1981).

FEDERAL ADMINISTRATIVE DECISIONS

Regular court opinions which consider administrative law questions are reported just as any other regular court cases. However, the legal decisions of administrative agencies as found in decisions of administrative law judges are quite another matter. Such decisions, according to the federal Administrative Procedure Act (Sec. 3b) and the Model State Administrative Procedure Act (Sec. 2a, 5) are to be publicly available, but an official comprehensive set of decisions in a format such as the West Reporter System for federal courts is not available. On the other hand, all federal agencies issue their own decisions, or are supposed to do so, in some format. Consulting two major sources we have put together a list of official federal administrative agency reports.[3]

Looseleaf Publications—Federal Decisions

Official agency sources are supplemented with unofficial looseleaf services published by private companies. These publications are designed for the subject specialist and are often expensive, ranging in annual cost from $100 to $600. Most looseleaf services are updated frequently and so can be useful for the presentation of up-to-date treatments of particular administrative law topics.

One encounters three different looseleaf formats; they are cumulative, interfiled, and monographic. The cumulative format simply places material updates next to the material that has come before it in time. Publications of the Bureau of National Affairs (BNA) usually take the cumulative form. The interfiled format replaces outdated materials with new substitutions. Old pages are literally deleted and new ones are added in their place. Commerce Clearing House (CCH) looseleafs are associated with this format. Monographic looseleafs look at first glance like ordinary books. Upon closer inspection, however, one finds a pressure binder system rather than the ordinary sewn or glued book binding. The pressure binding technique permits adding or supplementing pages at either the beginning or end of the text. The Matthew Bender and Company (MB) publishing house employs this last format.[4]

---

3. Johnson, *Federal Administrative Decisions*, 1 LEGAL REFERENCE SERVICE QUARTERLY 49–65 (1981); *A Uniform System of Citation*, 13th ed. (Cambridge, Ma.: Harvard Law Review Association, 1981), p. 135.

4. Berring and Wedin, *Looseleaf Services: A Subject Bibliography* 1 (4) LEGAL REFERENCE SERVICE QUARTERLY 51–53 (1981).

Table 1

Official Reports of Federal Administrative Decisions

Agency	Reporter Title	Dates Available
Agriculture: Decisions of the Secretary of Agriculture	Agriculture Decisions.	1942–
Alcohol, Tobacco and Firearms Bureau	Cumulative Bulletin. Quarterly Bulletin.	1972–78. 1972–
Atomic Energy Commission	Opinions and Decisions of The Atomic Energy Commission with Selected Orders.	1956–1975.
Civil Aeronautics Board	Reports.	1939–
Civil Service Commission	Appeals Decisions Index. Digest of Significant Decisions.	1975–78. 1974–78.
Defense Department	Digest of Decisions of the Armed Services Board of Contract Appeals. Digest of Decisions of the Corps of Engineers Board of Contract Appeals.	1942–56. 1946–72.
Employees Compensation Appeals Board	Decisions.	1946–
Energy Department	Federal Register.	1936–
Environmental Protection Agency (Office of the General Counsel)	A Collection of Legal Opinions. National Pollutant Discharge Elimination System Adjudicatory Hearing Proceedings: Decisions of the Administrator and Decisions of the General Counsel.	1970–73. 1974–76.
Environmental Protection Agency (Dept. of Agriculture, 1950–70)	Notices of Judgment Under the Federal Insecticide, Fungicide, and Rodenticide Act.	1950–
Federal Communications Commission	Decisions and Reports.	1934–
Federal Labor Relations Authority	Decisions and Interpretations of the Federal Labor Relations Council. Reports of Case Decisions. Digest and Tables of Cases of Decisions and Interpretations of the Federal Labor Relations Authority.	1970–78. 1979– 1979–

Agency	Reporter Title	Dates Available
Federal (U.S) Maritime Commission	*Decisions.*	1919–47, 1947–
Federal Mine Safety and Health Review Commission	*Decisions.*	1978–
Federal Power Commission	*Reports.*	1931–75.
Federal Reserve System	*Federal Reserve Bulletin.* *Digest of Rulings of the Board of Governors of the Federal Reserve System From 1914 to October 1, 1937.* *Published Interpretations of the Board of Governors of the Federal Reserve System.*	1915– 1914–1937. 1973–
Federal Services Impasses Panel	*Releases.*	1977–
Federal Trade Commission	*Decisions.* *Advisory Opinion Digests.*	1915– 1962–68.
Foreign Claims Settlement Commission	*Settlement of Claims.* *Decisions and Annotations.* *Index-Digest of Decisions.*	1949–55. 1950–1967. 1949–77.
General Accounting Office	*Decisions of the Comptroller General of the United States.* *Decisions.* (Advance Sheets). *Index-Digest of the Published Decisions of the Comptroller General of the United States.* *Civilian Personnel Law Manual.* *GAO Documents, Catalog of Reports, Decisions, Opinions, Testimonies and Speeches.*	1921– Monthly 1894–1976. 1977. 1975–
Health Care Financing Administration	*Rulings.*	1978–
Immigratioₙ and Naturalization Service	*Administrative Decisions Under Immigration and Nationality Laws.* *Interim Decisions.* *INS Reporter.*	1940– 1952–
Indian Claims Commission	*Decisions.*	1948–78.
Interior Department	*Decisions.* *Decisions.* (Advance Sheets) *Decennial Index-Digest of Unpublished Decisions.* *Index-Digest of the Department of the Interior.*	1881– 1955– 1943–54, 1955–64, 1965–74. 1975–

Agency	Reporter Title	Dates Available
	Pension and Bounty—	1887–1930.
	Land Claims Decisions.	1936–58.
	Grazing Decisions.	
	Opinions of the Solicitor of the Department of the Interior Relating to Indian Affairs.	1917–74.
Internal Revenue Service	*Treasury Decisions Under Internal Revenue Laws.*	1898–1942.
	Internal Revenue Bulletin.	1922–
	Internal Revenue Bulletin, Cumulative Bulletin.	1922–
	Bulletin Index-Digest System.	1953–78.
Interstate Commerce Commission	*Reports.*	1887–
	Motor Carrier.	1936–
	Valuation.	1918–64.
	Table of Cases and Opinions of the Interstate Commerce Commission.	1887–1921.
Justice Department	*Official Opinions of the Attorneys General of the United States.*	1789–
	Slip Opinions.	
	Digest of Official Opinions.	1921–58.
	Adjudications of the Attorney General of the United States.	1950–56.
Labor Department	*Opinions of the Solicitor for the Department of Labor Dealing with Workmen's Compensation.*	1908–15.
	Administrative Decisions Under the Walsh-Healey Public Contracts Act, Index-Digest.	1942–1964.
	Decisions and Reports on Rulings of Assistant Secretary of Labor for Labor-Management Relations Pursuant to Executive Order.	1970–1977.
	Digest and Index of Published Decisions of Assistant Secretary of Labor for Labor-Management Relations Pursuant to Executive Order 11491.	1970–
	Rulings on Requests for Review of the Assistant Secretary of Labor-Management Relations Pursuant to Executive Order 11491, as Amended.	1970–75.
Law Enforcement Assistance Administration	*Legal Opinions of the Office of General Counsel of the Law Enforcement Assistance Administration.*	1969–

Agency	Reporter Title	Dates Available
Maritime Subsidy Board (Dept. of Commerce)	*Decisions.*	1961–73.
Mine Operations Appeals	*Decisions of the Interior Board of Mine Operations Appeal.*	1970–78.
National Labor Relations Board	*Decisions of the National Labor Board.*	1933–34.
	Decisions.	1934–35.
	Decisions and Orders.	1935–
	Digest and Index of Decisions of NLRB.	1935–70.
	Classified Index of National Labor Relations Board Decisions and Related Court Decisions.	1970–
	Classified Index of Decisions of the Regional Directors of the National Labor Relations Board in Representative Proceedings.	1967–
	Classified Index of Dispositions of ULP (Unfair Labor Practices) Charges by the General Counsel of the National Labor Relations Board.	1967–
National Mediation Board	*Interpretation Issued by the National Mediation Board Pursuant to Section 5, Second of the Railway Labor Act.*	1934–76.
	Determination of Craft or Class of the National Mediation Board.	1934–
National Mediation Board (Emergency Board)	*Reports.*	1948–
National Transportation Safety Board	*Decisions.*	1967–
Nuclear Regulatory Commission	*Opinions and Decisions.*	1975–
	Preliminary Prints.	Monthly
Occupational Safety and Health Review Commission	*Administrative Law Judge and Commission Decisions.*	1971–
	Index Digest to OSAHRC Reports.	1971.
Patent and Tradmark Office	*Decisions of the Commissioner of Patents and U.S. Courts in Patent and Trademark Cases.*	1869–1968.
	Official Gazette.	1872–
Post Office	*Official Opinions of the Solicitor for the Post Office Department.*	1873–1951.

Agency	Reporter Title	Dates Available
Postal Rate Commission	*Opinion and Recommended Decision.*	1973–
Railroad Labor Board	*Decisions.*	1920–25.
Securities and Exchange Commission	*Decisions and Reports.* *Index to Commission Decisions.*	1934–
Social Security Administration	*Cumulative Bulletin.* *Social Security Rulings on Federal Oldage, Survivors, Disability, Supplemental Security Income and Miners Benefits.*	1960– 1960–
Subversive Activities Control Board	*Reports.*	1950–63.
Treasury Department	*Decisions of the First Comptroller.*	1880–94.
	Digest of Decisions of the Second Comptroller.	1817–94.
	Decisions of the Comptroller of the Treasury.	1880–1921.
	Digest.	1894–1920.
	Synopsis of Decisions.	1868–98.
	Treasury Decisions.	1899–1966.
	Customs Bulletin.	1967–
	Customs Bulletin and Decisions.	1967–
	Decisions/Rulings of U.S. Customs Service.	1978–
Veterans Administration	*Decisions.*	1941–55.
Veterans Education Appeals Board	*Selected Reports of Cases.*	1950–57.

There are hundreds of legal looseleaf services dealing with practically every legal subject. It would be impractical to list each of these services in a volume of this size. However, what we have done is to provide a list of looseleaf services that contain federal administrative decisions and rulings. This list is by no means complete but it does contain many administrative decisions which students of public administration will find helpful. Some of the listed services contain administrative decisions of state, local, and federal governments. Some contain digests of cases. Of general interest is the *Pike and Fisher Administrative Law Service*, a multivolume compendium in two series. It includes decisions from 6 appellate federal courts and 24 administrative agencies. However, it deals only with *procedural* aspects of the law.

STATE COURT REPORTERS

It is a mistaken view that only the national government is bureaucratic. The fact is that state and local governments have their own maze of complex regulations, rules, and judicial decisions. Agencies at the state level regulate much of daily activity. Licensing of businesses, employment, health and safety regulations, marriage, birth and death certification, education, zoning, and law enforcement are but a few life and death activities governed by state bureaucratic regulation. Indeed, the American federal system presupposes that the states will govern a large part of daily human interactions. The fact is that state courts are important policymaking centers independent of the federal judiciary. It falls to the state courts to define the boundaries of legitimate administrative activity at the state and local levels of government. Students of administrative law therefore must be knowledgeable of state court reporters and how to assess information from these sources.

Most states publish their own official court reports. Seventeen states no longer publish their own reports; they rely upon the reporter system published by the West Publishing Company.[5] It is this national reporter system that has made state appellate decisions available for all states and trial court opinions obtainable for some states. Most students will work with this massive set. The West Company has divided the nation into seven geographical regions. Following is a list of each regional reporter describing the states covered with a sample citation for each.

In addition to the regional reporters, the West Company publishes two specific state reports. The *New York Supplement* contains opinions delivered since 1888 of the New York Court of Appeals, all decisions of the Appellate Division of the Supreme Court, and all opinions of the lower courts of record. The *California Reporter* dates since 1960. It reports all decisions of the California Supreme Court, the California District Courts of Appeal, and the Appellate Department of the California Superior Court.

A relatively recent addition to the reporter system is the *Military Justice Reporter*. It contains decisions of the United States Court of Military Appeals and

---

5. Jacobstein and Mersky, *Legal Research Illustrated*, 2d ed. p. 53.

Table 2

Federal Administrative Decisions—Looseleaf Publications
(Selected List)

Subject Matter	Title	Publisher	Dates Available
Administrative Law (general)	Pike & Fisher Administrative Law.	Pike and Fisher	1952–
	Administrative Law.	Matthew Bender	1976–
Antitrust & Trade Regulation	Antitrust & Trade Regulation Reporter.	Bureau of National Affairs	1961–
	Trade Regulation Reporter.	Commerce Clearing House	1914–
Aviation	Aviation Law Reporter.	Commerce Clearing House	1931–
Carriers	Federal Carriers Reporter.	Commerce Clearing House	1937–
Copyright Law	Copyright Law Reporter.	Commerce Clearing House	1978–
Energy Regulation	Energy Users Report.	Bureau of National Affairs	1973–
	Federal Energy Regulatory Commission Reports.	Commerce Clearing House	1979–
	Nuclear Regulation Reporter.	Commerce Clearing House	1975–
	Oil and Gas Reporter.	Matthew Bender & Co.	1952–
Environmental Regulation	Chemical Regulation Reporter.	Bureau of National Affairs	1977–
	Environment Reporter.	Bureau of National Affairs	1970–
	Environmental Law Reporter.	Environmental Law Institute	1971–
	Noise Regulation Reporter.	Bureau of National Affairs	1974–
Food & Drug Regulation	Food, Drug, Cosmetic Law Reporter.	Commerce Clearing House	1938–
Government Contracts	Contract Appeals Decisions.	Commerce Clearing House	1956–
	Federal Contracts Reports.	Bureau of National Affairs	1964–
	Government Contracts Reporter.	Commerce Clearing House	1941–

Subject Matter	Title	Publisher	Dates Avail-able
Housing Regulation	*Equal Opportunity in Housing.*	Prentice-Hall	1973–
	Housing & Development Reporter.	Bureau of National Affairs	1973–
Labor Relations	*Labor Arbitration Reports.*	Bureau of National Affairs	1946–
	Labor Relations Reporter.	Bureau of National Affairs	1937–
	Labor Law Reporter.	Commerce Clearing House	1934–
	Public Employee Bargaining.	Commerce Clearing House	1977–
	Public Personnel Administration.	Prentice-Hall	1973–
	Government Employee Relations Report.	Bureau of National Affairs	1963–
Native Americans	*Indian Law Reporter.*	American Indian Lawyer Training Program, Inc.	1974–
Occupational Health & Safety	*Job Safety & Health.*	Bureau of National Affairs	1977–
	Mine Safety & Health Reporter.	Bureau of National Affairs	1979–
	Occupational Safety & Health Reporter.	Bureau of National Affairs	1971–
Poverty	*Poverty Law Reporter.*	Commerce Clearing House	1970–
Securities Regulation	*Blue Sky Reporter.*	Commerce Clearing House	1928–
	Federal Securities Law Reporter.	Commerce Clearing House	1933–
	Securities Regulation & Law Report.	Bureau of National Affairs	1969–
Social Security	*Unemployment Insurance —Social Security Reporter.*	Commerce Clearing House	1934–
Taxation	*Federal Tax Guide Reports—Control Ed.*	Commerce Clearing House	1958–
	Standard Federal Tax Reporter.	Commerce Clearing House	1913–
	Tax Court Reporter.	Commerce Clearing	1924–
	Federal Excise Tax Reporter.	Commerce Clearing House	1913–
Tobacco, Firearms, Explosives	*Tobacco, Firearms, Explosives Reporter.*	Commerce Clearing House	1978–

the Army, Navy, Air Force, and Coast Guard Courts of Military Review. *West's Bankruptcy Reporter* contains decisions from a variety of federal courts but is of limited utility for public administration students.

All West law publications contain a number of attractive reference features not found in official reports published by government. The Key Number System to be discussed later in this chapter under the Digest topic is a most important and valuable feature of West publications. The Key Number System coordinates all West publications, thus providing the researcher with an interlocking research network.

Table 3

Reporter	States Covered and Sample Citation
North Western Reporter 1879–1940 (1st series) 1940–present (2nd series)	Iowa, Michigan, Minnesota, Nebraska, North Dakota, South Dakota, Wisconsin. *Gibson* v. *Transportation Commission*, 315 N.W. 2d 346 (Wis. 1982).
Pacific Reporter 1883–1931 (1st series) 1931–present (2nd series)	Alaska, Arizona, California, Colorado, Hawaii, Idaho, Kansas, Montana, Nevada, New Mexico, Oklahoma, Oregon, Utah, Washington, Wyoming. *City of Roseburg* v. *Roseburg City Firefighters*, Local No. 1487, 639 P.2d 90 (Or. 1981).
Atlantic Reporter 1885–1938 (1st series) 1938–present (2nd series)	Connecticut, Delaware, Maine, Maryland, New Hampshire, New Jersey, Pennsylvania, Rhode Island, Vermont, and District of Columbia Municipal Court of Appeals. *Carol Lines, Inc.* v. *Pennsylvania Public Utilities Comm'n*, 439 A.2d 838 (Pa. Commw. 1981).
North Eastern Reporter 1885–1936 (1st series) 1936–present (2nd series)	Illinois, Indiana, Massachusetts, New York, Ohio. *Dotson* v. *Bowling*, 102 Ill. App. 3d 340, 430 N.E. 2d 44 (1981).
South Eastern Reporter 1887–1939 (1st series) 1939–present (2nd series)	Georgia, North Carolina, South Carolina, Virginia, West Virginia. North Carolina *State Bar* v. *DuMont*, 286 S.E. 2d 89 (N.C. 1982).
Southern Reporter 1887–1940 (1st series) 1940–present (2nd series)	Alabama, Florida, Louisiana, Mississippi. *Agrico Chemical Co.* v. *Department of Environmental Regulation*, 406 So.2d 478 (Fla. Dist. Ct. App. 1981).
South Western Reporter 1886–1940 (1st series) 1940–present (2nd series)	Arkansas, Kentucky, Missouri, Tennessee, Texas, Indian Territory. *Kentucky Commission on Human Rights* v. *Fraser*, 625 S.W. 2d 852 (Ky. 1981).

Looseleaf Services—State

Like federal administrative decisions, state administrative law decisions are available in looseleaf format. State court cases and state agency decisions will find their way into various looseleaf publications. The *All-State Sales Tax Reporter, State Tax Case Reporter, NOLPE School Law Reporter,* and *Workmen's Compensation Law Reporter* are merely a few looseleaf services focusing on state administrative law topics. And there are many more which resourceful students will want to consult in conducting searches for relevant materials. Check the library card catalog for looseleaf services that may be available locally.

LOCATING ADMINISTRATIVE RULES
AND REGULATIONS

Administrative rules and regulations do not appear systematically in court reporters. We have already discussed the availability of administrative decisions in both official and unofficial publication formats. But if the goal is to discern agency rules and regulations, and not necessarily the court review of these agency norms, the research task requires a different search technique. In the list appearing below we have recorded all U.S. jurisdictions with a register and administrative code. Although they may differ somewhat, each jurisdiction possessing these publications provides a relatively easy way to ascertain agency rules and regulations. For illustrative purposes, and because these are probably subject to the greatest usage by readers of this book, two U.S. government publications will be discussed. They are: the *Federal Register* and the *Code of Federal Regulations.*

Federal Register (Fed. Reg.)

Before 1936 much confusion existed over federal administrative rules and regulations. This was true because there was no centralized collection of them nor even a unified pattern of making them available to the public. This was changed by a much publicized court battle in 1935, in which the United States Attorney General brought suit based on a regulation that had been repealed previously (*Panama Refining Co.* v. *Ryan,* 293 U.S. 388). The following year Congress provided for a centralized listing of all agency rules and regulations, the *Federal Register.*

This series, now numbering hundreds of volumes, is published daily and all materials are arranged chronologically. The *Federal Register* contains newly adopted rules and regulations, notice of proposed regulations and rules, dates of administrative hearings, and presidential executive orders and proclamations. It is indexed monthly, quarterly, and annually. It should be noted that administrative decisions are not reported in the *Federal Register.* Such decisions are reported in the official agency reports or in the variety of unofficial reports discussed earlier in this chapter. A major difficulty with the *Federal Register* is that although it possesses indexes it does not contain a useful general index. This problem is remedied in another administrative law compendium, the *Code of Federal Regulations*.

Code of Federal Regulations (C.F.R.)

The *Federal Register* is arranged chronologically and not by subject. Therefore, it must be employed together with the *Code of Federal Regulations*. The *C.F.R.* is arranged under 50 separate titles and is published annually in pamphlet form. Because it is revised each year, the researcher can determine which rules and regulations are currently in force and which are not. The *C.F.R.* contains an easy-to-use annual index accompanied by monthly updates.

The *Code of Federal Regulations* together with the daily *Federal Register* should be used when attempting to update agency rules and regulations. After consulting the annual index to *C.F.R.*, the researcher should then turn to the monthly cumulative issue entitled, *LSA: List of CFR Sections Affected*. This procedure provides an up-to-date account for the year and month. However, rules and regulations are changed and promulgated on a daily basis so it is necessary to find the latest possible changes. This can be done by turning to the most recent daily *Federal Register*. Each *Register* contains a section titled, "Cumulative List of Parts Affected," a complete and current account of agency rules and regulations.

To illustrate the use of the *Federal Register* and the *Code of Federal Regulations* consider the following problem. You wish to locate the regulations, if any, governing cigarette smoking on public aircraft as of June 1, 1982. *Procedure*: Consult *CFR* index (as revised January 1, 1982). Look under appropriate headings. Under "cigars and cigarettes" you will find nothing of interest except the suggestion, "See also Smoking." Under that heading you will find one pertinent reference: "Aircraft, smoking aboard, 14 CFR 252." You subsequently turn to title 14 of the 1982 version of the *Code of Federal Regultions (CFR)* at part 252. There one finds the "final rule," which provides in substance that there must be smokers' and non-smokers' sections on passenger airplanes with 30 or more seats. It will also refer you to the regulation in the *Federal Register*, i.e., 45939, September 16, 1981. Consult also all the monthly issues available of the *List of CFR Sections Affected (LSA)* under the code designation Title 14, part 252—it reveals nothing new up to and including June 28, 1982. Then locate the copy of the *Federal Register* for September 16, 1981, and see the same final rule at the cited page. In addition, at pages 45934–45938 are a summary and supplementary information on the development of the final rule.

The following are sample citations for the *Federal Register* and the *Code of Federal Regulations*: Smoking Aboard Aircraft, 46 Fed. Reg. 45,934 (1981). If in the *Federal Register* it indicates where in *C.F.R.* the rule or regulation will appear, note it parenthetically; e.g., Smoking Aboard Aircraft, 46 Fed. Reg. 45,934 (1981) (to be codified at 14 C.F.R. § 252); Smoking Aboard Aircraft, 14 C.F.R. § 252.2 (1981).

State Registers and Administrative Codes

The listing below indicates that most state jurisdictions have registers and administrative codes parallel to that available for the U.S. government; some jurisdictions do not. This list was compiled initially by consulting a publication of the National Association of Secretaries of State.[6] The problem with relying on such a list is that it is quickly outdated. State legislatures from time to time hop on the administrative code bandwagon. We added a number of states to the roster of states with registers or administrative codes or both by consulting the card catalog in the law library. It is a method recommended for noting the existence of an administrative code for the state jurisdiction under investigation. Professor Elizabeth W. Matthews suggests that the student researcher look in the law library catalog under the subject heading, "DELEGATED LEGISLATION." This heading is subdivided by state, permitting one to determine if an administrative code exists for the jurisdiction in question.[7]

Researchers armed with these registers and codes may investigate particular state jurisdictions in depth or conduct comparative studies of state administrative rules and regulations. Both topics are fertile for intensive research.

LEGAL ENCYCLOPEDIAS

Encyclopedias are elementary research tools commonly employed by students in elementary school through college. Yet most students are unaware that legal encyclopedias are available and are convenient research tools.

Legal encyclopedias are of three varieties: general, local, and specialized. The general encyclopedias are most useful for public administration students. Encyclopedias dealing with local law and special subjects are of particular interest to the legal practitioner. Local law encyclopedias cover case and statutory law of a specific state but fewer than a third of the states have them. Special subject encyclopedias contain fairly comprehensive discussions of specific legal topics, such as automobiles, private corporations, or evidence.

The two general encyclopedias most often held by libraries are *American Jurisprudence 2d (Am. Jur. 2d)* and *Corpus Juris Secundum (C.J.S.)*. *American Jurisprudence 2d* replaces *American Jurisprudence*, and *Corpus Juris Secundum*

---

6. National Association of Secretaries of State, "State Administrative Codes and Registers: 1981/Federal Survey," mimeographed (Nashville, Tenn.: ACR Committee, 1981).

7. Elizabeth W. Matthews, *Access Points to the Law Library: Card Catalog Interpretation* (Buffalo, N.Y.: William S. Hein Co., 1982), p. 31.

Table 4

Administrative Registers and Codes

Jurisdiction	Register Name	Code Name
U.S. Federal Government	*Federal Register.*	*Code of Federal Regulations.*
Alabama	none	none
Alaska	none	*Alaska Administrative Code.*
Arizona	*Arizona Administrative Digest.*	*Arizona Official Compilation of Administrative Rules and Regulations.*
Arkansas	*Arkansas Register.*	none
California	*California Administrative Code Supplement.*	*California Administrative Code.*
Colorado	*Colorado Register.*	*Colorado Code of Regulations.*
Connecticut	*Connecticut Law Journal.*	*Regulations of Connecticut State Agencies.*
Delaware	*Delaware Documentation.*	*Register of Regulations.*
District of Columbia	*District of Columbia Register.*	*District of Columbia Municipal Regulations.*
Florida	*Florida Administrative Weekly.*	*Official Compilation Rules and Regulations of the State of Florida.*
Georgia	none	*Official Compilation Rules and Regulations of the State of Georgia.*
Hawaii	none	none
Idaho	none	none
Illinois	*Illinois Register.*	none (one in planning).
Indiana	*Indiana Register.*	*Indiana Administrative Code.*
Iowa	*Iowa Administrative Bulletin.*	*Iowa Administrative Code.*
Kansas	none	*Kansas Administrative Regulations.*
Kentucky	*Administrative Register of Kentucky.*	*Kentucky Administrative Regulations Service.*
Louisiana	*Louisiana Register.*	none (one in planning).
Maine	none	none
Maryland	*Maryland Register.*	*Code of Maryland Regulations.*
Massachusetts	*Massachusetts Register.*	*Code of Massachusetts Regulations.*
Michigan	none	*Michigan Administrative Code.*
Minnesota	*Minnesota State Register.*	*Minnesota Code of Agency Rules.*
Mississippi	none	none
Missouri	*Missouri Register.*	*Code of State Regulations.*
Montana	*Montana Administrative Register.*	*Administrative Rules of Montana.*

Jurisdiction	Register Name	Code Name
Nebraska	none	none
Nevada	none	none
New Hampshire	none, proposed in 1981.	none
New Jersey	*New Jersey Register.*	*New Jersey Administrative Code.*
New Mexico	*List of Rules and Publications Filed.*	none
New York	*New York State Register.*	*Official Compilation of Codes, Rules and Regulations.*
North Carolina	none	*North Carolina Administrative Code.*
North Dakota	none	*North Dakota Administrative Code.*
Ohio	*Ohio Monthly Record.*	*Ohio Administrative Code.*
Oklahoma	*The Oklahoma Gazette.*	none
Oregon	*Oregon Administrative Rules Bulletin.*	*Oregon Administrative Rules Compilation.*
Pennsylvania	*Pennsylvania Bulletin.*	*Pennsylvania Code.*
Rhode Island	*Compilation of Rules of State Agencies.*	*G.L. 42–35 General Laws of Rhode Island.*
South Carolina	*South Carolina State Register.*	*South Carolina Code of Regulations.*
South Dakota	*South Dakota Register.*	*Administrative Rules of South Dakota.*
Tennessee	*Tennessee Administrative Register.*	*Official Compilation-Rules and Regulations of the State of Tennessee.*
Texas	*Texas Register.*	*Texas Administrative Code.*
Utah	*State of Utah Bulletin.*	*Administrative Rules of the State of Utah.*
Vermont	*Vermont Administrative Procedures Compilation Bulletin.*	*Vermont Administrative Procedures Compilation.*
Virginia	*Register of Regulations of the Agencies of the Commonwealth.*	none
Washington	*Washington State Register.*	*Washington Administrative Code.*
West Virginia	*Rules and Regulations Division.*	none
Wisconsin	*Wisconsin Administrative Register.*	*Wisconsin Administrative Code.*
Wyoming	none	none

likewise supersedes the old *Corpus Juris*. Both *Am. Jur. 2d* and *C.J.S.* are publications of private companies which employ legal experts to write on various topics. They are not official government documents.

The encyclopedias contain articles on specific legal topics. These articles differ from a legal treatise or an article in a legal periodical in that there is no overt attempt to argue the merits of particular legal rules or principles. Instead the writers attempt to present clear, concise, and objective statements on the law of a particular topic. Both *Am. Jur. 2d* and *C.J.S.* are excellent tools for beginning research into a legal question. Besides an exposition on the law, the topical discussions are accompanied with cross-references to other legal research materials including, for example, cases, digests, statutory provisions, and annotations. Students will often want to go from the encyclopedia to the other cited sources for a more detailed understanding of the subject-matter.

American Jurisprudence 2d (Am. Jur. 2d)

Am. Jur. 2d is a discussion of both substantive and procedural aspects of American law arranged in more than 400 title headings. This particular encyclopedia places great emphasis upon federal statutory law and federal procedural rules. Students interested in detailed reference to state laws will be disappointed, although *Am. Jur. 2d* makes extensive references to the *Uniform State Laws*.

Public administration students will find most impressive and useful the scope of topics covered under the broad subject-heading "Administrative Law." It covers questions of jurisdiction, power, functions, and procedures of administrative agencies at all levels of government. In addition, *Am. Jur. 2d* contains expositions relating to agency investigatory, rule-making, adjudicatory functions, and much more. Administrative law matters are considered as well under other encyclopedia topics including: "Aliens and Citizens;" "Carriers;" "Commerce;" "Labor and Labor Relations;" "Licenses and Permits;" "Public Officers and Employees;" "Public Utilities;" "Taxation;" "Trademarks, Tradenames, and Unfair Trade Practices;" "Workmen's Compensation;" and "Zoning and Planning."

The volumes are arranged alphabetically by title. One might go directly to the titled volume, if already familiar with a particular legal topic. By reading the brief abstract and perusing the subject outline, the researcher can easily determine if he has turned to the appropriate discussion. This method, however, presupposes a sophistication probably lacking in most nonspecialist audiences, and it is probably necessary to refer to the General Index.

The simple procedures for using the *General Index* can be illustrated by an example. Suppose a term paper assignment calls for research on the eminent domain topic. Turning to the index item, "Eminent Domain," which appears in Volume D-E of the *General Index*, the researcher finds the entry on page 642. Because eminent domain is a many faceted topic, there are numerous subheadings spanning 51 pages of individual entries listed in alphabetical order from "Abandonment" to "Zoning and Planning." For illustrative purposes, let us stipulate that the topic has been narrowed to "eminent domain for the purpose of public highway construction." Scanning the subheadings under the index item "Eminent Domain" one finds on page 664 the subtopic, "highways and streets." This particular heading directs the researcher to a number of topic headings including: "generally, Em Dom §§ 45–48, 84, 119, 136, 150, 325–332." Be alert to the fact that the index is cross-referenced for easy access to substantive legal expositions, in our particular example to "Highways §§ 32, 33." If by chance one should at first encounter difficulties in locating an appropriate topic there is no need to despair. Try again; a suitable topic index entry will probably emerge with additional thought and effort. In fact, the more likely problem for the researcher is too many index items from which to choose.

After locating the correct entry in the *General Index*, the next step is to turn from the *Index* to the appropriate *Am. Jur. 2d* volume that contains the legal subject discussion. The abbreviation "Em Dom" obviously refers to the topic, eminent domain. However, a facile ability with the language will not suffice to discern all abbreviations found in this encyclopedia. The "Table of Abbreviations," which is located at the front of each volume of the *General Index*, has a list of abbreviations for each *Am. Jur. 2d* topic. Armed with a topic name, the student researcher should then look at the spine entries on each volume arranged in alphabetical order on the library shelf. Volume 26 is titled, "Elections §§ 183–394 to Eminent Domain §§ 1–246. Also note that Volume 27 carries Eminent Domain topics as well, "Eminent Domain §§ 247–506 to Escheat." The symbol (§) means section number and two symbols (§§) placed immediately next to each other refer to plural sections. In our particular illustration the topic items, Em Dom §§ 45–48, 119, 136, 150, 325–332 are located in Volume 26 and Volume 27. At page 700 of Volume 26 one finds § 45, "highways and streets." The search is now complete.

The legal exposition refers to original source material such as statutes, administrative rules and regulations, and case law. Secondary sources are also cited to other Lawyers Co-operative publications including annotations to *American Law Reports* discussed earlier in this chapter. *American Jurisprudence 2d* thus provides an excellent starting point for researching a legal subject. The following is a sample citation: 27 AM.JUR.2D *Eminent Domain* § 474 (1966).

Corpus Juris Secundum (C.J.S.)

Although probably not as useful for students of public administration as *Am. Jur. 2d*, *Corpus Juris Secundum (C.J.S.)* is also a massive statement of U.S. law. It totals over 100 individual volumes with more than 400 separate titles. This impressive encyclopedia includes references to reported cases decided as long ago as the seventeenth century. It has extensive references to state and federal law. Each subject essay is updated with an annual pocket supplement found in the back of each bound volume. Whole volumes are occasionally replaced with totally updated versions.

Written primarily for practicing attorneys, the publisher (West Publishing Company) has devised time-saving methods for finding the law on any given subject.[8] For the most part, the use of these methods presupposes a general knowledge of law not possessed by public administration students. Yet by employing similar elementary techniques as were described for *Am. Jur. 2d*, anyone can successfully use *Corpus Juris Secundum*.

A simple way to proceed is first to consult the five-volume *General Index* where, as one might expect, topics are listed in alphabetical order. By beginning with the most general title and then to the most specific sub-title, one can quickly focus on a particular subject. However, the *General Index* is designed to be used in conjunction with the title indexes to each *C.J.S.* subject matter title. Therefore, before turning to the specific subject essay, it is advisable to examine carefully the *Analysis* which appears at the beginning of each subject title. Thus the student should consult the appropriate volume of the encyclopedia itself for a detailed description of the subject matter discussed therein.

The *Analysis* briefly describes the nature of the topic and provides an outline of the general legal framework. In addition to legal essays, each volume has its own index. Moreover, at the back of each volume is a glossary of words, phrases, and legal maxims found there.

Two examples illustrate the research procedure. The first is relatively simple and straightforward; the second is designed to point out the difficulties that may be encountered.

First, let us say that we question whether prison officials may search inmate mail. Turning to the *General Index M–Q*, we find ''Prisons'' on page 777 and ending on page 783. Because there are numerous subheadings, we must narrow our investigation further. On page 782 you find: ''Searches and Seizures, prisoners' mail, Searches § 30.'' Having successfully narrowed the index search to the desired topic, we turn from the *Index* to the appropriate subject matter volume. Since ''Searches'' falls alphabetically within Volume 79—''Schools, etc. 323 to End—Sessions,'' Searches § 30 is located on page 798. Directly under the title heading, in bold print, is a brief statement on the general rule of law. A paragraph follows explaining applications of the rule with citations to a number of state and federal cases. We have also consulted the *Analysis* under Searches and Seizures and now are in a position to comprehend searches of prisoners' mail within the general context of search and seizure law.

The following example shows the many turns and bends one may employ in researching a particular question. Let us say that the question whether stare decisis applies to administrative decisions is raised and the instructor asks us to investigate and report our findings at the next class meeting.

We first refer to the *General Index A to Complex* under the subject heading, ''administrative law.'' But we learn immediately that the editors at the West Company have chosen not to publish separate expositions under the ''administrative

---

8. For a discussion of these methods see: *West's Law Finder: A Research Manual for Lawyers* (St. Paul, Minn.: West Publishing Co., 1980).

law'' subject-heading. Instead, the researcher is directed to ''Administrative Bodies and Procedures.'' But this heading, in turn, refers us to a number of subheadings which seem far off the research target. But our topic contains the words, ''stare decisis.'' Sure enough, at page 497 of the *General Index R-Z* we locate the heading, ''stare decisis,'' and its related subheading, ''administrative bodies.'' There in bold print is the *C.J.S.* topic, ''Publ Admin § 148.'' Finally on page 482 of Volume 73 *C.J.S.* we find it.

In bold print there is a brief statement on the general rule of law. A paragraph follows explaining the applications of the rule with citations to a number of state and federal court decisions and federal agency decisions. It is wise, *as it always is with legal reference materials*, to check the *Cumulative Annual Pocket Part* in the back of the volume for any changes in the rule or new decisions concerning the question. We have also consulted the *Analysis* under the topic heading, ''Public Administrative Bodies and Procedures.'' As a result, we are now ready to discuss intelligently the rule concerning stare decisis within the broader framework of administrative procedure. Perseverance will reap many rewards. The following is a sample citation for a footnote referencing *Corpus Juris Secundum*: 101A C.J.S. *Zoning and Land Planning* § 21 (1979).

CODES

Federal and state administrative codes have been discussed in the earlier chapter, but the world of codes is much broader, and the mastery of these sources is valuable to students of public administration and public law generally. In the United States there are federal, state, and local codes. Defined as systematic compilations of statutory law, most codes contain texts of statutes, constitutions, legislative histories, annotations to judicial decisions, various tables, and useful indexes. Students may have occasion to consult state and local codes, but they are so much like various federal codes, they do not need special treatment here.

There are three widely available federal codes: (1) *United States Code*, 1976 Edition (U.S.C.) as updated, including *Supplement IV (1980)*, is the official statement of the law; (2) *United States Code Service (U.S.C.S.)*; and (3) *United States Code Annotated (U.S.C.A.)*. The latter two are both commercial products of private companies but possess features not available in the official *United States Code*.

United States Code (U.S.C.)

Congress has codified United States law under 50 separate titles, e.g., Title 5, Government Organization and Employees; Title 13, Census; Title 39, Postal Service; Title 48, Territories and Insular Possessions. The four-part *General Index* is extensive, permitting the researcher to find the law quickly. There are also volumes titled *Popular Names and Tables*, which are useful for locating particular statutory laws within the *Code*. For example, the Administrative Procedure Act (APA) and its amendments may be found in a *Popular Names and Tables* volume listed in alphabetical order under "Acts Cited by Popular Name." The June 11, 1946, act is located there under Title 5, §§ 551–559, 701–706, 1305, 1306, 3344, 4301, 5335, 5352, 7521. The following is a sample citation for the official *United States Code*: 42 U.S.C. § 7407 (b) (Supp. IV 1980).

The *United States Code* contains sufficient information for searching U.S. statutory law. If *U.S.C.* is the only code available, it is sufficient for most tasks, but the unofficial codes possess features that make them even more useful.

United States Code Service (U.S.C.S.)

The *United States Code Service (U.S.C.S.)*, a publication of the Lawyers Co-operative Publishing Company (Bancroft-Whitney Company) is a remarkable research tool. Among its many features are the exact language from the *Statutes at Large*, legislative histories, annotations of interpretive case law, reference to relevant law review articles, an excellent five-volume *General Index*, and individual title indexes. This set also has an excellent two-volume annotation of the U.S. Constitution and a special two-volume set particularly useful for students of administrative law. The entire set is kept current through supplements inserted at the back of each appropriate volume.

The successor to the parent publication *Federal Code Annotated (F.C.A.)*, *U.S.C.S.* is arranged in the way of the official *U.S.C.* For example, the codification of law dealing with commerce and trade can be found under Title 15 in both the official *U.S.C.* and the unofficial *U.S.C.S.* Because most students will not be sufficiently familiar with the various official titles to turn directly to the code when starting research, they should consult the five-volume *General Index*. If, however, one knows the popular name of a law, for example, the "Sunshine Act," he or she should consult the special labeled-volume index containing popular names.

Extensive research aids are what make the *U.S.C.S.* so useful. It has, of course, the complete text of the relevant law. It refers to amendments and contains a complete research guide. It points out, for instance, where in the legal encyclopedia *American Jurisprudence 2d* a related discussion may be found. Its numerous annotations discuss how the law has been construed by judicial bodies. A very attractive feature is its bibliographic reference to law review articles on the various topics.

Administrative law students may benefit greatly from a special two-volume feature of this *U.S.C.S* set. Named *Administrative Rules of Procedure*, these volumes contain the rules promulgated by the following principal federal agencies for proceedings before them: Civil Aeronautics Board, Copyright Office, Equal Employment Opportunity Commission, Federal Communications Commission, Federal Maritime Commission, Federal Power Commission, Federal Trade Commission, Immigration and Naturalization Service, Internal Revenue Service, Interstate Commerce Commission, Maritime Administration, National Labor Relations Board, Occupational Safety and Health Review Commission, Patent Rules and Forms, Securities and Exchange Commission, Social Security Administration, and Trademark Rules and Forms. The Rules are printed as they appear in the official *Code of Federal Regulations*, and as amended and updated in the *Federal Register*. For example, on page 353 of the 1977 edition of the second volume of this set is an outline of the rules of practice of the Securities and Exchange Commission—this as it appears in 17 CFR §§ 201, 202, 203. By turning a few pages one also comes across the verbatim rules, useful research guides containing relevant law review articles, interpretative notes, and judicial decisions.

The two volume set dealing with the Constitution's articles and amendments is an additional feature of *U.S.C.S.* which deserves mention. These volumes contain many of the research aides included in the Code. For instance, under Article I, section 1, one finds the exact wording of the constitutional provision, cross references to *Am.Jur.2d*, essays on the delegation of legislative authority topic, law review articles, interpretative notes, and court decisions on this central administrative law topic.

All in all, *U.S.C.S.* is a most valuable statement of U.S. codified law. With its various aids of particular usefulness for students of administrative law, this source should be examined by all students of the subject. Remember, always consult the cumulative supplements at the back of these bound volumes—a rule to be followed with all legal research materials. Materials from *U.S.C.S.* should be cited as follows: 42 U.S.C.S. § 7407 (b) (Law. Co-op. 1982).

United States Code Annotated (U.S.C.A.)

The West Publishing Company issues the *United States Code Annotated (U.S.C.A.)*. Better known and more widely employed than *U.S.C.S.*, it also annotates relevant judicial interpretations and features collateral references to the many other West publications. This fine set contains an eight-volume index and a multiple volume treatment of each provision of the U.S. Constitution. As with *U.S.C.S.*, the *General Index* or *Popular Name Index* is the best way to research a statutory topic.

Research may be updated by consulting the pocket supplements of each volume or the separate paperback volumes which are cumulative supplementary pamphlets published occasionally to keep *U.S.C.A.* current. Finally, always consult the last published pamphlet of the *U.S. Code Congressional and Administrative News*. This West publication cumulates the changes in statutory law since the publication of *U.S.C.A.* pocket supplements and the latest *Supplementary Pamphlet(s)*. Here is a sample *U.S.C.A.* citation: 42 U.S.C.A. § 7407 (b) (West 1981 Supp. Pamph.).

DIGESTS

A digest is an available research tool designed to find cases on a particular legal topic without reading all the reported cases in American law. Digests are necessary because of the way court decisions are reported, which is to say chronologically instead of by topic. In essence, a digest is an index to the reported cases according to subject matter, providing brief abstracts of the facts or holdings in a case. Unlike an encyclopedia, it does not present a narrative on the law with accompanying footnotes. Instead, it is a research aid that seeks out the cases dealing with particular facts or legal problems. Because the digest is only an index, it is always necessary to proceed to the actual court decisions.

The ability to identify all the relevant cases, decisions, or rules on a given administrative law topic is—to understate the accomplishment—a valuable time saver. Digests are published to accommodate a variety of needs. Administrative rulings are available in abbreviated form in digests; they are often found in conjunction with administrative decisions outlined earlier in this chapter. Of particular interest is the Pike and Fisher, *Administrative Law Service*, a multi-volume compendium in two series which is supplemented by a looseleaf service. It includes decisions from 6 appellate Federal courts and 24 administrative agencies, but it deals only with the *procedural* aspects of the law. A national digest is available if a researcher is interested in all reported cases in U.S. jurisdictions, and should he be interested in only a particular part of the country, there are regional editions. Digests are also available for a number of state jurisdictions and the District of Columbia. We will describe the West digest system for all of American law and for the more specialized court systems; the regional and state digests are segments of the national digest and are used the same way.

American Digest System

The American Digest System is a colossal work consisting of more than 350 volumes. It is a subject classification of all reported cases appearing in West Publishing Company's *National Reporter System*. The first set of this digest system, known as the *Century Digest*, covers the period from 1685 to 1896. For each succeeding ten-year period there are decennial digests from the *First Decennial* (1897–1906) to the *Eighth Decennial* (1966–1976). Beginning with the two-part *Ninth Decennial*, the period covered is of five years' duration (1976–1981). For the period since 1981, the *American Digest System* is supplemented by the *General Digest*. The *General Digest* in the past was supplemented by monthly paperback issues which were eventually bound in hardcover. At present, because of improved publishing technology, each supplement is hardbound and given a permanent volume number. All the abstracted cases are arranged according to the West Publishing Company "Key Number System."

Key Number System is West's scheme for assigning cases or sections of cases to appropriate subject categories. This system first divides the law into seven main classes. Each class is then divided into subclasses and then each subclass is divided into topics. The topic, "Administrative Law and Procedure," is located under the seventh main class, "Government," and within the subclass, "Systems and Sources of Law." The topics are further divided into subdivisions. Finally, a Key

Number is assigned to each subdivision.[9] Importantly, the researcher is in the position to locate all reported cases on a particular topic by first identifying the appropriate topic and key number. By examining each *Decennial* and *General Digest* all the cases on a given topic may be identified. There is a variety of approaches which may be employed to use the Key Number System. Only two, however, are best suited for nonlawyer researchers: the *Table of Cases Index*, and the *Descriptive-Word Index*.

The *Table of Cases Index* approach may be illustrated by way of a concrete example. After reading the Supreme Court's decision in *Elrod* v. *Burns* (1976), the topic of party patronage and freedom of association may emerge, along with an interest in identifying all reported cases dealing with political patronage and public employment. Each *Decennial* and *General Digest* contains an alphabetical listing of cases by plaintiff, in our example: *Elrod*. Because *Elrod* v. *Burns* was decided by the U.S. Supreme Court in 1976, the *Table of Cases Index* for the *Eighth Decennial* is employed. Upon finding *Elrod* v. *Burns* the researcher first encounters its legal citation (96 SCt 2673), followed in turn by the various Topic and Key Numbers under which the case has been digested: i.e., Civil R 13.2 (4); Const Law 67, 68(1), 72, 82, 91, 274.1(2); Offic 18, 66. After settling upon one or more of the listed Topics and Key Numbers, it remains only to consult each *Decennial* and *General Digest* for a complete abstract of all relevant cases.

The *Descriptive Word Index* is a second and sometimes quicker tool for locating Topics and Key Numbers. While this approach is less time consuming than the case index method, it requires more thought. There is a separate *Descriptive Word Index* for each unit of the *Decennial* and *General Digest*. Each volume in the *Sixth Series* of the *General Digest* contains its own *Descriptive Word Index* and *Table of Cases Index*. By thinking first of a "magic word," or catch word, the student may then consult the *Descriptive Word Index* to determine whether such an entry exists. "Patronage" is an obvious magic word for cases involving the doctrine found in *Elrod* v. *Burns*. In most cases, however, selecting the right word will prove more difficult. One need not despair after failing on the first or second attempt; a huge number of word entries is present. Try additional "magic words." Sooner or later the desired reference will be found.

With the appropriate Topic and Key Number identified, it may be reported, with reasonable confidence, that the relevant case law has been located. That is, the digest system has provided the index of all West reported cases on the specific problem under investigation. Moreover, public administration students will find the various Digest topics familiar ground. Names, headings, classes, and topics such as "administrative law," "eminent domain," "counties," "securities regulation," and "zoning" are much in evidence.

It must be emphasized again that the West Publishing Company has devised a variety of ways and means to find the desired cases. But these methods were

---

9. Ibid., pp. 13–20. Also see: Jacobstein and Mersky, *Fundamentals of Legal Research*, 2d ed., pp. 67–82.

created for those who possess extensive legal training or experience. We recommend therefore the *Table of Cases Index* and the *Descriptive Word Index* approaches because these tools do not require advanced legal training. Simply working with them will build confidence.

Specialized Digests

The West Publishing Company issues a number of state, regional, and federal digests in addition to the *American Digest*.[10] It is important to note that each of these specialized digests is a segment of the *American Digest System*. Consequently, if one has access to the parent *American Digest System*, there really is no great need to consult the more specialized digests. Reflecting particular academic interests, college libraries may hold one or more of the specialized digests but not the *American Digest System*. Administrative law students interested in only federal law or in only opinions of the U.S. Supreme Court will find *Federal Practice Digest, 2d* and the *U.S. Supreme Court Digest* adequate.

Federal Practice Digest, 2d. This is the digest to use if the topic is confined to federal case law. Because it is a West publication, *Federal Practice Digest, 2d* also employs the Key Number System. If the purpose is to understand the corpus juris (body of law) of the entire federal judicial system, this digest is the proper tool because it includes all reported cases of the federal district courts, courts of appeal, and the U.S. Supreme Court. Its special features include paragraphs indicating whether a case has been affirmed, reversed, or modified, and references to secondary sources such as *Corpus Juris Secundum*.

Federal Practice Digest 2d indexes cases since 1961; for earlier cases (1939–1961) one must consult *Modern Federal Practice Digest*; for still earlier cases (1754–1938), the *Federal Digest* should be used. The set is kept current by annual pocket supplements and pamphlet supplements.

U.S. Supreme Court Digest (West Publishing Company). The *U.S. Supreme Court Digest* contains only digests of U.S. Supreme Court decisions. It also employs the Key Number System and duplicates the cases found in the *American Digest System* and the *Federal Practice Digest, 2d* series. It is kept up to date by cumulative annual pocket supplements. This 25-volume digest is ideal for research projects requiring only U.S. Supreme Court decisions.

U.S. Supreme Court Reports Digest: Lawyers' Edition. This digest of U.S. Supreme Court opinions is published by the Lawyers Co-operative Company and the Bancroft-Whitney Company. This is the same publishing outlet that

---

10. The regional digests correspond to the regional reporter system of the West Publishing Company. The regional digests are: *Atlantic Digest, North Western Digest, Pacific Digest, South Eastern Digest,* and *Southern Digest.*

markets *American Jurisprudence, 2d*, and *United States Code Service*. Because it is not a West publication, it does not employ the Key Number System. Nevertheless, the *U.S. Supreme Court Reports Digest* is easy to use and contains both a *Table of Cases* and a *Word Index*.

The *Table of Cases* lists U.S. Supreme Court decisions under both plaintiff and defendant names. It also presents the popular names under which cases are sometimes known. Beneath the alphabetical listing for each case, the full case citation is given, followed by the topic and section number(s) under which each case is digested. Rather than going directly to the digest topic and number designation, it is advisable to consult first the scope-note and outline preceding each topic title. The scope-notes define the subject parameters of each topic. For example, the case of *Consolo* v. *Federal Maritime Commission*, 383 U.S. 607 (1966) is digested under five different topics, i.e., Administrative Law, Appeal and Error, Costs and Fees, Damages, and Shipping. As is common for all digests, the editors abstract cases under a number of different topics. Choosing the topic title of greatest research interest can be achieved by carefully studying the scope-notes and outlines before reading each of the digest entries. By so doing, the researcher can save time and considerable effort.

The *Word Index to U.S. Supreme Court Reports Digest: Lawyers' Edition* is utilized in the same way as West's *Descriptive Word Index*. Mentally run through those "magic words" relevant to subject matter. If at first you do not succeed, try again. There are thousands of words from which to choose. After some practice, this method will become second nature.

As with most legal research material, the *Supreme Court Reports Digest: Lawyers' Edition* is kept current by pocket supplements inserted at the back of each bound volume. The supplements should always be consulted.

CITATORS

A citator is an additional tool that locates the law. It is designed to determine quickly how cited cases have been treated by subsequent court decisions. Has a particular case been sustained? Overruled? Modified by a later court decision? Thus it is possible to learn the current status of a rule of law determined many years ago.

All the citators are published by Shepard's Citations, Inc., now a division of McGraw-Hill. Just a few uses of citators are: U.S. Supreme Court cases; lower federal court cases; state court cases; criminal justice cases; federal labor law; federal administrative agency decisions; federal regulations; patents and trademarks; and law reviews. *Shepard's United States Citations: Cases; Shepard's United States Administrative Citations; Shepard's Acts and Cases By Popular Name; Shepard's United States Citations: Statutes;* and *Shepard's Code of Federal Regulations Citations* are five specialized citators with which students of public administration should be familiar.

Shepard's United States Citations: Cases

Typically, upon opening the maroon cover of one of the huge volumes in this set, the initial feeling is one of intimidation. What seems to be an immense blur of tiny legal citations placed on very thin pages hits home with a wallop. But, like most legal research material, the citator actually is easy to use.

The starting point is a legal citation to a court case and a need to locate those cases that cite a given case in a significant fashion. Because sometimes a researcher has a citation for only one of the reporting systems, Shepard's Citations, Inc. reserves separate sections of each volume for each of the three parallel citations for each case: *United States Reports* (U.S.); the unofficial *Lawyers' Edition* (L.Ed.); or West's unofficial *Supreme Court Reporter* (S.Ct.). Beginning with a citation to a particular case (for example, 295 U.S. 495), one locates the volume number of the citation (295) at the upper corner of each printed page of the citator. Because the volume numbers are arranged numerically, this is an easy task. On the body of each page, printed in bold numerals, is the page number of each case (in our example, 495). The desired case is first located by volume and page number, which, once done, clears the way for locating the citing cases.

Because a case citation is included when a judge cites a case in his written opinion, the number of citations is often great. The result of this editorial decision is to list a citing case whenever a judge mentions a cited case, even vaguely or incorrectly. Reading each of these cited cases would be an enormous task, and so the editors have provided cues whenever a cited case has been treated in a significant manner—when a case is distinguished or overruled, for example. These cues are presented in the form of lower and upper case letters appearing at the left edge of the cited or citing cases. These letters are abbreviations for, among other things, explanations of how the court case was cited.

A complete listing of the abbreviations and definitions is provided in each volume. The cues can be noted on the left edge of the columns. To determine the context and language used by the court in its decision, the researcher should then read the citing case in either the official or unofficial reports.

The famous "Sick Chicken" case can illustrate the use of *Shepard's United States Citations: Cases*. After reading *A.L.A. Schechter Poultry Corp.* v. *United States*, 295 U.S. 495 (1935) you reach the reasonable conclusion that the U.S. Supreme Court has held, at least in part, that Congress may not delegate its legislative authority to the President. However, you also know that since 1935 Congress has "delegated" much authority to the President. You are troubled by an obvious threshold query: Has the Supreme Court reversed its "Sick Chicken" decision, has it modified, distinguished, or explained its 1935 opinion? It occurs to you that the Court may have had no occasion to rule on a question of delegation since 1935. For a quick fix, you turn to *Shepard's United States Citations: Cases*.

With the official case citation in hand, the research process may begin. The official citation for the "Sick Chicken" case is 295 U.S. 495. It is observed that Volume 1B, part 2 of *Shepard's United States Citations: Cases* has citations for

Supreme Court cases reported in volumes 151–313 of *United States Reports (U.S.)*. Because the case citations are arranged in numerical order, you find 295, the volume number of *U.S.* in which *Schechter* is reported—and there, on page 3064 of Volume 1B, part 2, is located 295 U.S. 495.

Under the cited case page entry 495 the parallel citations to the case are located: 79LE 1570; 55SC 837; and 97 ALR 947. Immediately below and following these citation entries are several citations to cases describing the judicial history of the "Sick Chicken" case. At the left hand margin are the editor's notations or cues in the form of lower case *s* and lower case *f*. The letter *s* indicates that the federal court case is the same case as the case cited. The letter *f* signifies that the case is cited as controlling.

This sequence of entries is followed by a heading titled: "Commerce." But you know that the commerce clause issue in this particular case is only one of several and you are concerned with another issue, namely, delegation of legislative power. So you continue to search through the headings until you find on page 3065: "Legislative Power—Delegation." And there you also find a column-long listing of cases in which *Schechter* has been cited. In the left hand margin of this column you find the editor's cues. The cues or notations include *d, j, f,* and *e*. These designations indicate that *Schechter* was distinguished (*d*) from the case at bar; or explained (*e*), which means that the importance of *Schechter* was discussed in the case at bar; or followed (*f*), meaning that it was cited as controlling in the case at bar. You also observe the lack of an "*o*", an indication that *Schechter* has not been overruled.

Because Shepard's Volume IB contains cases up to the year 1943, it is necessary to consult additional volumes and supplements to the current year. Turning to the *1943–1971 Supplement to Case Edition 1943* we find on page 747 numerous citations and editor notations, but once again no cue indicating that *Schechter* has been overturned. We repeat this same process with all the supplements through June 1982, finding that the decision in *Schechter* has not been overruled. You properly conclude that an understanding of the delegation principle may best be ascertained by reading those cases in which the "Sick Chicken" case is distinguished (*d*) and explained (*e*). Judges may choose to ignore unwelcomed precedents by distinguishing the facts of a present case from the facts of previous cases; a strict interpretation of precedent is one way judges exercise discretion.[11] You understand that to explain what the court "really meant" in its previous opinion is but a variation of the skillful task of judicial decisionmaking.

Shepard's United States Administrative Citations

Presently appearing in two volumes and supplemented in paperback updates, this source is a comprehensive presentation of all citations to official department-,

---

11. Karl Llewellyn, *The Bramble Bush* (New York: Oceana Publications, 1930), pp. 66–69.

court-, board-, and commission-reported decisions of federal administrative bodies. *Shepard's United States Administrative Citations* contains references divided in the following manner:

Opinions of the Attorneys General of the United States
Decisions of the Department of the Interior, Public Lands
Decisions of the Department of the Interior
Treasury Decisions
Protest Review Decisions
Abstracts (Board of General Appraisers)
Abstracts, New Series (Customs Court)
Reappraisement Decisions
Application for Review Decisions
Customs Rules Decisions
Valuation Decisions
Abstracted Protest Decisions
Abstracted Reappraisement Decisions
Abstracted Valuation Decisions
Court of Customs Appeals Reports
Court of Customs and Patent Appeals Reports (Customs)
Custom Court Decisions
Treasury Decisions, Internal Revenue
United States Board of Tax Appeals Reports
Tax Court of the United States Reports
United States Tax Court Reports
Interstate Commerce Commission Reports
Valuation Reports
Motor Carrier Cases
Federal Communications Commission Reports
Federal Power Commission Reports
Federal Trade Commission Decisions
Securities and Exchange Commission Decisions and Reports
American Maritime Cases

How is this valuable citator used? Let us say that the researcher is concerned with the question arising in the appellate case of *Eldon L. Smith* decided by the Interior Board of Land Appeals (Dept. of Interior) on April 18, 1972. The case was an appeal from several decisions by a district manager denying applications for grazing licenses until damages for a grazing trespass had been paid. The case itself appears in Volume 79 of *Decisions of the United States Department of Interior* at page 149. To determine how this case has been subsequently treated, one would go to Part 1 of *Shepard's United States Administrative Citations*, which includes decisions of the Department of the Interior; on page 117 is found the reference to Volume 79 of the *Decisions of the United States Department of Interior*, and then the page number 149, indicating that the case does appear. There is, however, only one reference: "cc 78ID55," which means that in Volume 78 of the *Decisions of the Department of the Interior* at page 55 is a "connected case" which is a "different case from case cited but arising out of same subject matter or intimately connected therewith." You learned this from the abbreviation analysis which appears on pages XIV–XV in the front of the Shepard's volume. Then, use the same Shepard's volume to analyze that case (cc 78ID55), which directs attention to Volume 78, p. 55. There two references are found; one is to the starting point, cc 79ID149, the other to 78ID135. This means that on page 135 of Volume 78 of the *Decisions of the Department of Interior* is yet another pertinent case to be found. This is checked in the same Shepard's volume, but we find no reference there. However, the bound volumes are kept up to date by use of paperback supplements. Of the three cases cited above, only one, 79ID1149, is in the July 1982 supplement. Under that heading there are two citations: 84ID479 and 86ID671. Neither of these appears to have been cited, and we have, therefore, come to the end of our search. For the present we have a handle on all references to the original case. However, the supplement (Shepard's) is a cumulative quarterly, so if the research is conducted after the October quarterly issue has been published, the search would need to be accordingly updated.

Shepard's Acts and Cases by Popular Names

This citator lists alphabetically those federal and state acts and cases that have been cited by popular name. So, if only the popular name is known but not the desired citation to an act, *Shepard's Acts and Cases By Popular Names* is the source to consult. Suppose a student reads a popular magazine article that asserts that the U.S. Administrative Procedure Act requires that people who appear before an agency are entitled to be represented by legal counsel. Two questions arise: (a) in what particular section of the APA does such a provision exist; and (b) how has that provision been interpreted by the courts? The researcher has no citation to the APA, only its popular name.

Beginning with the popular name, "Administrative Procedure Act," one turns to *Shepard's Acts and Cases by Popular Names* and finds the reference on page 14 to the *U.S. Code 1976* Title 5, § 551 et seq., 701 et seq. Then upon consulting Title 5 in the *U.S. Code* itself one finds that the provision for legal counsel is provided in § 555(b) of the APA. To answer the second part of the query, the researcher must next analyze Title 5 § 555(b) in *Shepard's United States Citations: Statutes*.

Shepard's United States Citations: Statutes

The *Statutes* edition of *Shepard's United States Citations* contains citations to: *U.S. Constitution; United States Code; United States Code Annotated; Federal Code Annotated (USCS); United States Statutes at Large; United States Treaties and Other International Agreements; General Orders in Bankruptcy*, and court rules for a number of courts including the U.S. Supreme Court.

This multi-volume set with supplements has a variety of references including citations to court decisions. To answer the question of how courts may have interpreted section 555(b) of the Administrative Procedure Act one turns to that section of the citator containing the *United States Code*. First, one runs through the numbered titles to reach Title 5. Then one looks down the columns until he or she reaches section number 555, and then subsection b. At that point there are references to over 30 cases. In the most recent supplement there are additional case references.

Shepard's Code of Federal Regulations Citations

Finally, assume that the student's research concerns a regulation, in this instance Title 8, § 334.11 of the *Code of Federal Regulations(CFR)*, which has to do with "petition for naturalization and preliminary application." In this particular situation one turns to a volume called *Shepard's Code of Federal Regulations Citations*. The volume includes citations to the *Code of Federal Regulations*, presidential proclamations, and executive orders. Under the first of these the search turns to Title 8, and then § 334.11. Under that heading there is only one citation, 155 FS. 429, and there is none in the most recent paperback supplement. This reference leads to one U.S. District Court case, "Matter of the petition of Andreas Vacontios," decided September 30, 1957. (The citation to page 429 indicates the exact page where § 334.11 of Title 8 is cited; the exact citation of the case, however, is 155 FS. 427). To search the citations for that Federal District Court case, yet another member of the Shepard family is used, *Shepard's Federal Citations*; and indeed, there are two references under the citation 155FS. 429—and so on.

LEGAL PERIODICALS

The periodical literature on administrative law is scattered widely in the law journals, not localized in a few specialized publications. There are, however, some specialized publications that may be described as follows. The sole journal devoted to administrative law is the *Administrative Law Review*, a quarterly published since 1949 by the Administrative Law section of the American Bar Association (ABA).[12] In addition, *Regulation*, published bimonthly since 1977 by the American Enterprise Institute, focuses on administrative law but covers related concerns as well. Also there are a number of newsletters devoted to the subject. The exact number is uncertain, but the ABA, for instance, has published a newsletter quarterly since 1974 called *Administrative Law News*, and the Illinois Bar Association has published *Administrative Law* since 1972 with three to six issues per year.

A series of articles by Bernard Schwartz (the latest entitled "Administrative Law Cases During 1982"), which has been published annually since 1972 in the *Administrative Law Review* is the best device for keeping abreast of the latest legal

---

12. From 1949 to 1959 it was titled, *Administrative Law Bulletin*.

developments. A promising tool for the practicing or academic public administrator is the projected quarterly, *The Public Administrator and the Courts*, to be supplemented by a casebook and a cumulative index. Only one issue (July, 1981) has been published to date, however, and its future is not yet clear.

Also, a number of journals are concerned with specific facets of administrative law. Among these, the following:

I.C.C. Practitioner's Journal
Institute on Securities Regulation
Arbitration Journal
Bulletin of the Copyright Society of the U.S.A.
Copyright Law Symposium
Ecology Law Quarterly
Environmental Law
Food Drug Cosmetic Law Journal
Harvard Environmental Law Review
J.A.G. Journal
Journal of the Patent Office Society
Military Law Review
Natural Resource Journal
Planning, Zoning and Eminent Domain Institute
Public Law
Securities Regulation Law Journal

In approaching the periodical literature the initial point is overriding, i.e., the literature is found in a wide spectrum of law and other social science and public administration journals. To locate this literature the student should consult inter alia, the *Index to Legal Periodicals* (after 1926) and its predecessor, the *James-Chapman Index to Legal Periodicals* (1886–1937). Such general indexes as *Facts on File*, the *Guide to Periodical Literature*, and *Sage Public Administration Abstracts* should not be overlooked. The *Index to Foreign Legal Periodicals* is an indispensable comparative law source. Finally, the *Index to Periodical Articles Related to Law* is very helpful.

Index to Legal Periodicals

The most exhaustive index of legal periodicals published in the United States is the *Index to Legal Periodicals*, issued by the H.W. Wilson Company. Beginning in 1908, this index contains articles appearing in legal journals in the United States, Canada, Great Britain, Ireland, Australia, and New Zealand. For articles published before 1908, there is the *James-Chipman Index to Legal Periodicals*—a six-volume set for the period 1888–1937.[13] The *Index to Legal Periodicals* has four main features: (1) subject and author index; (2) table of cases; (3) table of statutes; and (4) book review index.

---

13. Jacobstein and Mersky, *Fundamentals of Legal Research*, 2d ed., p. 315.

Subject and Author Index. A *List of Subject Headings* is contained in each cumulative volume and supplement. The researcher should first determine the subject heading that best describes the research topic. If interested in articles dealing with medical proof in workmen compensation suits, one can find in the *List of Subject Headings*: "Workmen's compensation: medical aspects." Numerous articles can be located by first turning alphabetically to "Workmen's Compensation," and then to the subheading—"Workmen's Compensation: medical aspects."

Locating entries is slightly more complicated when seeking a particular author. First, one locates in alphabetical order the author's last name. Under this is a list of subject headings under which the author's article(s) is classified. Turning to the appropriate subject heading(s) the author's name and article title are easily noted. Depending on the scope of the research project, it is advisable to consult a number of past and current volumes and to check the paperback supplementary indexes.

Following the article listings under each subject heading, case notes or discussions of recent cases relevant to the subject classification are listed when available under the title, "Cases." For instance, in Volume 20 (September 1980 to August 1981) following the list of articles under the subject heading, "Estoppel," there is a list of four case notes dealing with the topic. It first lists the case, followed by the name of the law journal, volume, page, and date of publication in which the case is discussed. These case notes, varying in length from a few to many pages, are often very helpful in determining what a particular case might mean.

Table of Cases Commented Upon. Besides the listing of case discussions under the separate subject headings, there is the handy *Table of Cases Commented Upon*. Located immediately behind the *Subject and Author Index*, it lists each case alphabetically by plaintiff name; this is followed by the law journal entries. If the assignment is to find what has been written about a particular case, this table is a quick and ready source.

Table of Statutes Commented Upon. This is located immediately behind and performs the same task as the above mentioned *Table of Cases Commented Upon*. Each statute is listed alphabetically by its name followed by its legal citation, followed in turn by lists of articles that discuss or comment upon the statute.

Book Review Index This separate section of the *Index to Legal Periodicals* lists book reviews on legal subjects by name of author or, if the author's name is unknown, by title.

Current Law Index

A relatively new index, sponsored by the American Association of Law Libraries and published by the Information Access Corporation, *Current Law Index* (CLI), made its debut in 1980. More than 660 periodicals are referenced and, in addition to the usual citations, it contains a few novel features. When cited in an article, statutes are indexed by both their popular and official names. Books are graded in the book review section on a scale of A to F according to the evaluation of the reviewer. *CLI* is updated with supplements.

Index to Foreign Legal Periodicals

This tool locates articles dealing with International Law, Comparative Law, and Municipal Law of non-common law countries. The *Index to Foreign Legal Periodicals* contains article listings from 1960 to the present and contains author, subject, geographical, and book review indexes. It is published by the Institute of Advanced Legal Studies of the University of London in cooperation with the American Association of Law Libraries.

Articles that appear in legal periodicals are cited differently from those featured in social science journals. Example: Braeman, *Overview of FOIA Administration in Government*, 34 AD. L. REV. 119 (1982).

Index to Periodical Articles Related to Law

This index was created in 1958 to meet the growing recognition among lawyers of a need to apply the social and behavioral sciences to law. It includes English language articles of research value but which do not appear in the *Index to Legal Periodicals* or the *Index to Foreign Legal Periodicals*. The *Index to Legal Periodical Articles Related to Law* is published quarterly and has a subject index, an index to articles, and an author index. It lists published articles of legal significance but which appear in journals not normally concerned or associated with legal topics. References under "Administrative Law and Procedure," cover articles on the American scene, while articles under "Administrative Law and Procedure," followed by a national designation, are helpful for comparative administrative law. There is also a cross-referenced section on "ombudsman" which is useful.

LAW DICTIONARIES

Most law dictionaries define a word or phrase in its legal sense and give citations to court decisions or their references. In this sense, law dictionaries are elementary research tools. A law dictionary can be useful, although often an expensive acquisition.

Two widely known and employed law dictionaries are: (1) Ballentine, *Law Dictionary with Pronunciations*, 3rd edition, Lawyers Co-operative Publishing Company, 1969; and (2) Black, *Law Dictionary*, 5th edition, West Publishing Company, 1979. Two excellent, less technical and less expensive dictionaries are: Gifis, *Law Dictionary*, Barron's Educational Series, Inc., 1975; and Oran, *Law Dictionary for Non-Lawyers*, West Publishing Company, 1975.

Students may want to consult Chapter 6 of this volume for often-encountered words and phrases in the administrative law field.

COMPUTER-ASSISTED LEGAL RESEARCH

One should be aware of the existence of new electronic devices for data retrieval. Three such systems exist from which a variety of materials discussed in this chapter may be obtained. They are known as: LEXIS, WESTLAW, and AUTO-CITE. LEXIS is a service provided by Mead Data Central of New York City; WESTLAW is a product of the West Publishing Company of St. Paul, Minnesota; and AUTO-CITE is produced by the Lawyers Co-operative Publishing Company in Rochester, New York.

The data base for each service differs with each providing useful legal research material. With commands of key names, concepts, terms, words, cases, authors, or judges, for example, the computer will respond by printing out the desired material. This computer terminal centered process may be employed both to verify research conducted manually and or to conduct the entire research project while seated at a computer terminal. Of course, those who want to use these time-saving services must consult a specially trained and designated law librarian or have access to a school or to a law firm office which subscribes to one of the computer services.

It must be emphasized that computer-assisted legal research is not a substitute for learning how to use the law library. The computer systems rely on what is already in published form and placed on library shelves. Also, none of the computer services contains all library materials. Consequently, one cannot intelligently give computer commands without first understanding the organization and functions of legal research materials. In any event some research materials simply are not yet available on the computer.

LEGAL RESEARCH EXERCISES

Actually working with legal research materials is the best teacher. The following exercises are designed to provide students with a successful ''hands-on'' learning experience. Correct answers for the exercises are provided at the end of the chapter.

Exercise #1—Legal Encyclopedias

For questions 1–3 use *C.J.S.*
You are interested in airport zoning.
1. Employing the *General Index, R–Z*, where is the researcher directed?
2. Employing the *General Index, A to Complex*, to find references on airport zoning, to what index are you directed?
3. May a conditional use permit be granted to airports?
For questions 4 and 5 use *Am. Jur. 2d*.

4. Is a special zoning permit generally necessary to constuct an amateur radio or television tower in a residential district? Give title and section citation.
5. Has the U.S. Supreme Court decided any case concerning the issue raised in question 4?

Exercise #2—Legal Codes

For question 1 use *U.S.C.*
1. How does Title 15, section 1701 define the word "Person"?

For questions 2 and 3 use *U.S.C.S.*
2. Where may a discussion of zoning powers in Guam be found?
3. What Public Law grants to the Legislature of Guam authority to undertake urban renewal?

For questions 4 and 5 use *U.S.C.A.*
4. What is the name for Title 48?
5. What is the *C.J.S.* cross-reference to Title 48, section 1425?

Exercise #3—Digests

For questions 1 and 2 use the *First and Second Decennial Digest.*
1. Use the *Descriptive Word Index.* What key name and number deals with Public Land Grants to colleges and universities? (Think in terms of "magic words.")

Use the response to question 1 to answer question 2.
2. What 1905 Florida case held that the Legislature has the power to prescribe what college or colleges shall be the recipient or recipients of the interest on the funds derived from the sale of lands donated by an Act of Congress?

Use the *Fourth Decennial Digest* to answer question 3.
3. How many cases are listed under the exact Key Name and Number of the answer for question 1?

Use West's *Federal Practice Digest 2d* for question 4.
4. Employing the *Table of Cases*, under what Key Name(s) and Number(s) is the case of *Equal Employment Opportunity Commission* v. *Zia Co.* found?

Use *U.S. Supreme Court Digest: Lawyers' Edition* for question 5.
5. The case is *Frey and Sons* v. *Cudahy Packing Co.* Under what topic(s) and number(s) is the case listed?

Exercise #4—Citators

1. What are the parallel citations for the case, *United States* v. *DuPont* 353 U.S. 586 (1957)?
2. Which case questions the soundness of the *DuPont* decision? (Give citation only.)

3. Between 1971 and 1976, which U.S. Supreme Court decision "explained" the *DuPont* decision? (Give citation only.)
4. As of 1980, has the *DuPont* decision been overruled?
5. What is the meaning of the following citation—91 FTC 286?

Exercise #5—Legal Periodicals

For questions 1 to 4, use the *Index to Legal Periodicals*.

1. Between August 1949 and July 1955 how many articles were written on zoning regulations and the right of a doctor to use his home as an office? (Check titles only, no need to read articles.)
2. Between August 1949 and July 1955 list the articles written by Samuel W. Eager, Jr.
3. What does the abbreviation SALJ stand for?
4. Between August 1949 and July 1955, how many case comments have been written on *Cain* v. *U.S.*, 211 F 2d 375?
5. Use the *Ten Year Index to Periodical Articles Related to the Law*. Under what subject index (headings) is there an article on Philippine corporate law?

ANSWERS FOR LEGAL EXERCISES

Exercise #1—Legal Encyclopedias

1. See Title Index to Zoning and Land Planning
2. See Title Index to Zoning and Land Planning
3. Yes
4. No; Zoning, section 176
5. No

Exercise #2—Legal Codes

1. " 'person' means an individual, or an unincorporated organization, partnership, association, corporation, trust, or estate." (p. 1435)
2. Title 48, section 1425a
3. Nov. 4, 1963, P.L. 88–171, Title 1, 77 Stat. 304.
4. Territories and Possessions
5. C.J.S. Territories, sections 18, 19

Exercise #3—Digests

1. Colleges and Universities, 4
2. *State* v. *Bryan*, 39 So. 929, 50 Fla. 293
3. O (none, no paragraph)
4. Fed Cts 944
5. App., sections 1585L, 1673 q; ev, sections 979e, i; Tr, section 172 b.

Exercise #4—Citators

1. 77 Sup. Ct. 872; 1 L.Ed. 2d 1057
2. 237 FS 891
3. 420 U.S. 241
4. No
5. Volume 91 of the *Federal Trade Commission Decisions*, page 286

Exercise #5—Legal Periodicals

1. 1
2. *Constitutionality of the Proposed Appointment of an Ambassador to the Vatican*, 16 ALBANY L. REVIEW 208 (23 June 1952)
3. SOUTH AFRICAN LAW JOURNAL
4. 1
5. Corporations-Philippines

4

A Survey of the Literature

If legal research were nothing more than a search for cases supplemented by use of codes, statutes, digests, and the like, it would be a sterile exercise. A comprehensive view of the law requires perusal of a wide scope of literature. The present list is an introduction to such scope, but only an introduction, a guide to further literature. In addition, the final chapter of this book is a comprehensive bibliography including many older volumes.

Here is a selection of books likely to be available in general university and college collections supplemented by law library holdings. The listings are in designated categories to facilitate use, but the categories are not themselves topical. Most of these sources have brief annotations. While some works are self contained and relatively timeless, the researcher must keep his work thoroughly contemporary.

MAJOR TREATISES, TEXTS, AND CASEBOOKS

The works in this section range from single volume general texts and casebooks to multi-volume treatises. All are general and comprehensive. Only recent works are listed here; earlier texts are found in Chapter 7, Selected Bibliography.

A few words of general description: (a) Casebooks are compilations of past litigation. They are particularly useful for tracing the case-by-case development of a particular facet of law. While many instructors find them acceptable as the sole text for a course, others see them as being short on explanation and long on confusing detail. But often casebooks contain both cases and commentary, which gives them greater utility. (b) The few really comprehensive treatises in administrative law are of great value in giving detailed explanations for most facets of the law. Primarily, these are library sources and should be available. (c) Finally the texts, several of which include some abridged cases, emphasize both continuity and explanation. A useful inquiry can often begin with the commentary in a text or treatise, but such a source must be seen for what it is—a dated beginning.

Administrative Law in the American Political System. Kenneth F. Warren. St. Paul: West Publishing Co., 1982.

A recent comprehensive text written by a political scientist for social science students. An excellent commentary containing edited cases and a superb glossary.

Public Law and Public Administration. Phillip Cooper. Palo Alto, Calif.: Mayfield Publishing Co., 1982.

A public law text written specifically for students of public administration. A particularly important and useful appendix is devoted to state administrative law, broken down state by state.

Administrative Law. 6 vols. Basil J. Menzines, Jacob A. Stein, Jules Gruff. New York: Matthew Bender, 1981.

This is a loose leaf multi-volume compendium, kept up to date with inserts. Published since 1977, it is concerned primarily with the national scene. Its scope is comparable to Davis' *Treatise.*

The Legal Foundations of Public Administration. Donald D. Barry, Howard R. Whitcomb. St. Paul: West Publishing Co., 1981.

A course text focused on the processes by which policy is changed into law and applied by agencies. It contains cases, readings, and questions, but is primarily a commentary.

Administrative Law Treatise. 2d ed., 3 vols. Kenneth Culp Davis. San Diego, Calif. K. C. Davis Publishing Co., 1978, 1979, 1980.

The premier treatise on American administrative law, it is thorough and comprehensive.

Administrative Law Cases and Comments. 7th ed. Walter Gellhorn, Clark Byse, Peter L. Strauss. Mineola, N.Y.: The Foundation Press, 1979.

The latest edition of a distinguished comprehensive compilation of cases, readings and author commentary.

Administrative Law: A Casebook. Bernard Schwartz. Boston: Little Brown and Co., 1977.

A substantial comprehensive teaching work containing both cases and notes.

Administrative Law: Cases and Materials. 4th ed. Louis L. Jaffe and Nathaniel L. Nathanson. Boston: Little, Brown and Co., 1976.

A lengthy comprehensive teaching volume containing cases, notes, questions, and commentary.

Administrative Law. Bernard Schwartz. Boston: Little, Brown and Co., 1976.

A major and substantial comprehensive textbook. It is a commentary.

Legislative and Administrative Processes. Hans A. Linde and George Bunn. Mineola, N.Y.: The Foundation Press, Inc., 1976.

A general textbook written by two political scientists primarily for use by other than law schools.

Administrative Law and Government. 2d ed. Kenneth Culp Davis. St. Paul: West Publishing Co., 1975.

Unlike other Davis texts, this one is designed for undergraduates and is oriented toward liberal education. The chapters on discretion are especially useful.

Text-Cases-Problems on Administrative Law, Regulation of Enterprise, and Individual Liberties. Edwin Wallace Tucker. St. Paul: West Publishing Co., 1975.

This is a text focused on business education. It deals with the roles and procedures of administrative agencies with a business school perspective.

Administrative Law Text. 3d. ed. Kenneth Culp Davis. St. Paul: West Publishing Co., 1972.

One of several major works by the author of *Administrative Law Treatise* noted above; primarily a comprehensive law school text.

Administrative Agencies and the Courts. Frank E. Cooper. Ann Arbor: University of Michigan Law School, 1951.

A systematic, general treatise on administrative law which, consistent with its date of publication, focuses on the main administrative agencies.

An Introduction to Administrative Law with Selected Cases. 2d ed. James Hart. New York: Appleton-Century Crofts, Inc., 1950.

One of the earlier general and comprehensive texts with cases on administrative law.

The Law of Administrative Tribunals. 2d ed. E. Blythe Stason. Chicago: Callaghan and Co., 1947.

An early text on general administrative law.

OFFICIAL STUDIES, REPORTS

Listed in this section are a few seminal studies or reports that have resulted from congressional or executive assessments of crucial aspects of national administrative procedure.

The Administrative Conference of the United States.

Since 1964 this conference has sponsored many studies or inquiries, all of which are published and available. Convenient summaries appear in Baley, *Administrative Conference of the United States: A Selected Bibliography 1968–1980,* 33 AD. L. REV. 235–253 (1981). Also see: 30 AD. L. REV. 303 (1978).

Manual for Administrative Law Judges. Merritt Ruhlen. Washington: Government Printing Office, 1974.

Prepared for the administrative conference of the United States, this little manual sketches the procedures available to an administrative law judge.

Attorney General's Manual on the Administrative Procedure Act. Prepared by the United States Department of Justice. Reprinted by Holmes Beach, Fla.: William W. Gaunt & Sons, Inc., 1973.

A reprint of the first edition published by the U.S. Government in 1947, it is a guide to the meaning and application of the Federal APA.

A New Regulatory Framework: Report on Selected Independent Regulatory Agencies. [U.S.] President's Advisory Council on Government Organization. Washington: U.S. Government Printing Office, 1971.

A government report that recommends some marked changes in agency structure, including abolition of the FTC and replacement of collegial commissions in several other agencies with single administrators.

Task Force Report on Legal Services and Procedures. [U.S.] Commission on Organization of the Executive Branch of the Government. Washington: U.S. Government Printing Office, 1955.

This is the task force report on legal services and procedures of the so-called 2d Hoover Commission. Among other things, it considers public information, rule-making, adjudication, licensing, hearings, judicial review, and an assortment of matters pertinent to administrative jurisprudence.

Task Force Report on Regulatory Commissions. (Rept. #14 [Appendix N]). U.S. Commission on Organization of the Executive Branch of the Government. Washington: U.S. Government Printing Office, 1949.

This is the report of the 1st Hoover Commission's Task Force dealing with the following nine regulatory agencies: U.S. Maritime Commission, the Civil Aviation Board, the Interstate Commerce Commission, the Federal Communications Commission, the Federal Power Commission, the Federal Reserve Board, the Federal Trade Commission, the National Labor Relations Board, and the Securities and Exchange Commission.

The Hoover Commission Report. [U.S. Commission] on Organization of the Executive Branch of the Government. New York: McGraw Hill Book Co., Inc., (n.d.).

A commercial printing of the 1949 Hoover Commission Report, it includes under one cover not only material on the regulatory agencies but also on the other task force reports.

Administrative Procedure in Government Agencies. [U.S.] Monograph [s] of the Attorney General's Committee on Administrative Procedure. (S. Doc. #10, 77th Cong., 1st sess.). Washington, D.C.: U.S. Government Printing Office, 1941.

Fourteen staff studies of administrative procedure embracing the Wage and Hour Division and the Children's Bureau (Department of Labor); Social Security Board; the National Railroad Adjustment Board and the National Mediation Board; National Labor Relations Board; Civil Aeronautics Authority; Department of the Interior; United States Employees' Compensation Commission; Bureau of Internal Revenue, Board of Tax Appeals, and Processing Tax Board of Review; Bituminous Coal Division (Department of the Interior); Interstate Commerce Commission; Federal Power Commission; Securities and Exchange Commission; United States Tariff Commission and Bureau of Customs.

Administrative Procedure in Government Agencies. [U.S.] Final Report of the Attorney General's Committee on Administrative Procedure. (S. Doc. #8, 77th Cong., 1st sess.). Washington, D.C.: U.S. Government Printing Office, 1941.

This major governmental study focused on agency procedure and led ultimately to the Federal Administrative Procedure Act. It contains a wealth of detail.

Report of the Committee with Studies of Administrative Management in the Federal Government. [U.S.] President's Committee on Administrative Management. Washington, D.C.: U.S. Government Printing Office, 1937.

This report is one of the older official government studies of the executive branch and its agencies. It is critical of the existence of agencies outside of the departments and of the existence of a "4th branch" of government.

GOVERNMENTAL INFORMATION SOURCES

Here are a number of books of particular value in locating an office, a function, or a particular official. They can be used to supplement the *U.S. Government Manual*, state "Blue Books," and like compendia. Similarly, one may find comparable (but rarely detailed) information on the states in state "Blue Books" and similar sources, as noted elsewhere in this book. For cities, a directory, if available, can be most helpful.

American Politics Yearbook, 1982–83. Jarol B. Manheim. New York: Longman, 1982.

A remarkably compact sourcebook listing names, addresses, functions, and key personnel in governmental agencies and departments as well as in the Congress. It identifies leading political issues and attributes them to departments, agencies, and congressional committees. There is also a valuable interest group section.

Washington Information Directory 1981–82. Mary M. Neumann, ed. Washington: Congressional Quarterly, Inc., 1981.

This research tool by the publisher of *C.Q. Weekly Report* and other materials contains a wealth of descriptive material on the Washington scene. It includes data on the executive agencies, Congress, and nongovernmental organizations.

Encyclopedia of Governmental Advisory Organizations. 3d ed. Linda E. Sullivan, ed. Detroit: Gale Research Co., 1980.

This volume contains the names, addresses, phone numbers, histories, programs, memberships, staffs, and meetings for advisory committees of the federal government. It is divided into 10 functional areas from agriculture to transportation.

The National Directory of State Agencies 1980-1981. Nancy D. Wright and Gene P. Allen, Herner and Company, compilers. Arlington, Va.: Information Resources Press, 1980.

This is the fourth biennial edition. It contains alphabetical listing of state agency functions, ranging from adjutant general to worker's compensation; state government telephone information numbers and addresses; state agencies listed alphabetically by state; state agencies by functions; and an appendix which lists the names and addresses and phone numbers of associations of state government officials.

Federal Regulatory Directory 1979-80. Robert E. Healy, ed. Washington: Congressional Quarterly, Inc., 1979.

An annual publication, it includes general material on government regulations and information on the specific agencies and departments. The information includes background, procedures, organization, personnel, telephone numbers, functions, and a wealth of detail on each.

MATERIALS ON STATE & LOCAL ADMINISTRATIVE LAW

In this section are a few works which should help orient the student to state aspects of administrative law. Besides these works, there is an appendix on state administrative law materials found in Cooper's *Public Law and Public Administration*, annotated here under Major Treatises, Texts, and Casebooks.

The Book of the States, 1982-1983. Vol. 24. Jack L. Gardner, ed. Lexington, Ky.: The Council of State Governments, 1982.

The latest volume in a series published by the Council of State Governments, it is a good starting point for organizational and statistical data about state governments.

Administrative Codes and Registers: 1981 State/Federal Survey. William N. Bates/National Association of Secretaries of State, Administrative Codes and Registers Committee. Nashville: ACR Committee, [1981].

A listing of each state's code and register together with pertinent basic data as of August, 1981. But note a caution and supplementation in Chapter 3.

State Government Reference Publications: An Annotated Bibliography. 2d ed. David W. Parish. Littleton, Colo.: Libraries Unlimited, Inc., 1981.

A common problem encountered in the study of state government is the difficulty in locating materials. While other source materials exist—most notably the U.S. Library of Congress Monthly Checklist of State Publications—few furnish the depth of coverage and organization provided by David Parish. The book is divided into nine chapters: Official State Bibliography; Blue Books; Legislative Manuals and Related References; State Government Finances; Statistical Abstracts and Other Data Sources; Directories; Tourist Guides; Audiovisual Guides, Atlas, and Maps; and Bibliographies and General References.

The National Directory of State Agencies 1980-1981. Nancy D. Wright and Gene P. Allen, (compilers). Arlington, Va.: Information Resources Press, 1980.
     See notation under GOVERNMENTAL INFORMATION SOURCES, above.

Ombudsman Papers: American Experience and Proposals. Stanley V. Anderson. Berkeley: Institute of Governmental Studies, University of California, 1969.
     Although there is national material included, state and local ombudsman proposals and experiences are predominant in this work. A large bibliography.

The Law of Urban Affairs: Cases, Problems, Materials. 2 vols. Norman Redlich. New York: New York University School of Law, 1968.
     This work was compiled for the "exclusive use of students at the New York University School of Law," but it has application to the administrative law needs of city administrators and for any student of such problems.

State Administrative Law. 2 vols. Frank E. Cooper. Indianapolis: Bobbs-Merrill Co., Inc., 1965.
     One of a very few major works of comprehensive character on the administrative law of the American states. Since it touches all states it is particularly valuable; unfortunately it is somewhat dated.

Administrative Law and Local Government. Bernie R. Burris. Ann Arbor: University of Michigan Law School, 1963.
     A brief but useful application of the principles of administrative jurisprudence to local government. It is particularly pertinent to local government officials.

Administrative Adjudication in the State of New York. Robert M. Benjamin. [No publisher or place of publication], 1942.
     An early work on state administrative law, it is an official study designed to investigate the execution of quasi-judicial functions by state boards, commissions, and departments.

SOME HISTORICALLY SIGNIFICANT WORKS

The few works noted here, and several found in the Selected Bibliography (Chapter 7), are of use in pinning down the earlier reservations expressed about the whole concept of administrative law. Some of these were concerned with whether administrative law was not a violation of the constitutional principle of separation of powers, and therefore inappropriate. Others emphasized the importance of regular court review of administrative agency actions. Still others chart the earlier reactions from which contemporary usage and acceptance has emerged.

The Constitution of Liberty. Friedrich A. Hayek. Chicago: University of Chicago Press, 1966.

Part II of this work includes a clear acknowledgement of the value of appropriately circumscribed administrative law and of administrative courts, contrary to many accounts of Hayek's opposition to them.

Introduction to the Study of the Law of the Constitution. 10th ed. E. C. S. Wade and A. V. Dicey. London: Macmillan, 1959.

The classic work by Dicey containing his famous critique of the French *Droit Administratif.* This critique is the same as the version which first appeared in the 7th edition of 1908. It is considerably less severe than the version in earlier editions.

Administrative Law. Roscoe Pound. Pittsburgh: University of Pittsburgh Press, 1942.

This little volume of five lectures is concerned with remedying defects in judicial overview of administrative law, with the intent to assure appropriate guarantees of fair play.

Bureaucracy Triumphant. Carleton Kemp Allen. London: Oxford University Press, 1931.

One of the important critiques of administrative law as it was developing in England a half century ago.

The New Despotism. The Rt. Hon. Lord [Gordon] Hewart. London: Ernest Benn Limited, 1929.

This work by the then Lord Chief Justice of England is one of the classic negative critiques of administrative law in British legal literature.

Administrative Justice and the Supremacy of Law in the United States. John Dickenson. New York: Russell & Russell, Inc., 1927.

A famous expression of a traditional critical view of administrative law.

Legislative Functions of National Administrative Authorities. John Preston Comer. New York: Columbia University Press, 1927.

One of the earlier works placing in meaningful perspective the legal aspects of the administrative process.

The Principles of the Administrative Law of the United States. Frank J. Goodnow. New York: G. P. Putnam's Sons, 1905.

The first text published in the United States purporting to be on United States administrative law. It is a sort of sequel to the author's comparative administrative law (noted elsewhere in this chapter), but in modern terms it is as much a treatise on public administration and the executive branch as on administrative law per se.

THE REGULATORY AGENCIES

Much of the emphasis of administrative law has traditionally centered upon the regulatory agencies, i.e., those agencies set up to control crucial aspects of the economy. The few works listed here, together with their bibliographies, will lead the student into this area. These agencies include the Civil Aeronautics Board, the Federal Communications Commission, the Federal Maritime Commission, the Federal Power Commission, the Federal Trade Commission, the Interstate Commerce Commission and the Securities and Exchange Commission, sometimes called the "big seven."

Smoking and Politics. 3d ed. A. Lee Fritschler. Englewood Cliffs: Prentice Hall, Inc., 1983.
A case study of the process and law of the cigarette labeling controversy.

The Federal Trade Commission Since 1970: Economic Regulation and Bureaucratic Behavior. Kenneth W. Clarkson and Timothy J. Murris, eds. New York: Cambridge University Press, 1981.
An unfavorable critique of the FTC, with some suggestions for reform including tighter judicial oversight and adjudication by the regular courts rather than by the FTC.

Regulating Business: The Search for an Optimum. Chris Argyris [and associates]. San Francisco: Institute for Contemporary Studies, 1978.
Essays by eleven contributors on the regulation of various aspects of the economy.

Governance of Federal Regulatory Agencies. David M. Welborn. Knoxville: University of Tennessee Press, 1977.
This is a study of the formulation of policy, internal management, and organization of the "big seven" regulatory agencies—the Civil Aeronautics Board, the Federal Communications Commission, the Federal Maritime Commission, the Federal Power Commission, the Federal Trade Commission, the Interstate Commerce Commission, and the Securities and Exchange Commission. There is a useful bibliography.

Working on the System. James R. Michael, ed. New York: Basic Books, Inc., 1974.
This is "a comprehensive manual for citizen access to federal agencies" by Ralph Nader's Center for Study of Responsive Law. It is lengthy and comprehensive.

The Economic Regulation of Business and Industry. 5 vols. Bernard Schwartz, ed. New York: Chelsea House & R. R. Bowker, 1973.

This multi-volume work is essentially a detailed legislative history of the American regulatory agencies. Contains a wealth of detail and documentation.

Federal Administrative Proceedings. Walter Gellhorn. Baltimore: Johns Hopkins Press, 1941 (reprinted Westport, Conn.: Greenwood Press, 1972).

In this relatively early work the writer sees the administrative agency and its law as a reasonable approach to many problems of modern government. He does not share the fears of many contemporaries that processes differing from the traditional ones of the courts are necessarily dangerous.

The Supreme Court and Administrative Agencies. Martin Shapiro. New York: The Free Press, 1968.

A study of the relationship between the courts and the agencies and their similarities and differences. There is a special focus on the patent office, by way of example.

The Administrative Process. James M. Landis. New Haven: Yale University Press, 1966 (Greenwood reprint, 1974).

One of a few brief and relatively early works on the modern focus of administrative law. Appearing first under the Storrs Lecture Series at Harvard, it emphasizes the viability of administrative agencies endowed with quasi-legislative and quasi-judicial powers and with a measure of independence based on their expertise.

Judicial Control of Administrative Action. Louis L. Jaffe. Boston: Little, Brown, 1965.

One of the important commentaries on administrative law centering upon the thesis that the courts and agencies form a "partnership" in regard to both the making and the applying of law.

Administrative Law: The Informal Process. Peter Woll. Berkeley: University of California Press, 1963.

This short book by a political scientist is largely concerned with the adjudicative activities of agencies.

The Professor and the Commissions. Bernard Schwartz. New York: Alfred A. Knopf, 1959.

Deals with the author's experiences as a controversial chief counsel for the House Special Subcommittee Investigating the Federal Regulatory Agencies. The focus is on six major agencies.

Federal Examiners and the Conflict of Law and Administration. Lloyd D. Musolf. Baltimore: The Johns Hopkins Press, 1952 (published in The Johns Hopkins University Studies in Historical & Political Science Series LXX, No. 1).

This study considers the problem of the administrative judge (then called "examiner") whose role was not sufficiently differentiated, in the view of some critics.

The Federal Administrative Procedure Act and the Administrative Agencies. George Warren, ed.; Introduction by Arthur T. Vanderbilt. New York: New York University School of Law, 1947.

A publication of the papers delivered at an institute held at New York University. It deals with the first Federal APA passed in 1946.

The Independent Regulatory Commission. Robert E. Cushman. New York: Oxford Universtiy Press, 1941. (Reprinted by N.Y.: Octagon Books, 1972).

A treatment of the most important regulatory agencies, it stems from its author's experience on the staff of the President's Committee on Administrative Management, but is not confined by those parameters. It includes much historical and comparative (British) data.

ADMINISTRATIVE DISCRETION

One of the newer questions of administrative jurisprudence centers upon the control of discretion. Much of the concern has to do with police discretion, but in reality the problem permeates all of administrative law. The works listed here will introduce a substantial part of the literature beginning with Davis' 1969 study.

Working the Street: Police Discretion and the Dilemmas of Reform. Michael K. Brown. New York: Russell Sage Foundation, 1981.

This is an inquiry into the factors contributing to the discretionary decisions made by police officers. It is based on a study of three California communities.

Police Discretion. Kenneth Culp Davis. St. Paul: West Publishing Co., 1975.

The pioneering study of police discretion and selective enforcement.

Law and Bureaucracy: Administrative Discretion and the Limits of Legal Action. Jeffrey L. Jowell. Port Washington, N.Y.: Dwellen Publishing Co., Inc., and Kennikat Press Corp., 1975.

A study of administrative discretion, which centers on data from the Massachusetts Commission on Discrimination, the Boston Department of Welfare, and the Boston Redevelopment Authority.

Administrative Discretion. Clark C. Havinghurst, ed. Dobbs Ferry, N.Y.: Oceana Publications, Inc., 1974.

Six articles that succeed Davis' *Discretionary Justice.* They deal with decisional referents, confining administrative discretion, review of contract awards, SEC, no action records, presidential spending discretion, and discretion in military justice.

Discretionary Justice, A Preliminary Inquiry. Kenneth Culp Davis. Baton Rouge: Louisiana State University Press, 1969.

A now classic treatment of the position that "[t]he vast quantities of unnecessary discretionary power that have grown up in our system should be cut back, and the discretionary power that is found to be necessary should be properly confined, structured, and checked."

THE "LEGISLATIVE" COURTS

The tribunals discussed in the works listed here are or were originally administrative courts in principle, yet they are usually considered separately. They are listed here because they are broadly appropriate to the study of administrative law even though they figure only peripherally in most administrative law studies. Legislative courts derive from authority other than Article III of the Constitution, and are not restricted to judicial functions.

A Brief History of the United States Court of Customs and Patent Appeals. Giles S. Rich. Washington: [Superintendent of Documents], 1980.
    A volume authorized by the Committee on the Bicentennial of Independence and the Constitution of the Judicial Conference of the United States. It is written by a judge of the Court and contains much historical and biographic information.

The United States Tax Court: An Historical Analysis. Harold Dubroff. Chicago: Commerce Clearing House, Inc., 1979.
    A very well documented account of the function and development of the Board of Tax Appeals, established in 1924, which ultimately (in 1969) became the U.S. Tax Court.

The United States Court of Claims: A History Part I: The Judges 1855-1976. Marion T. Bennett. Washington: [Superintendent of Documents], 1976.
The United States Court of Claims: A History Part II: Origin—Development—Jurisdiction, 1855-1978. Wilson Cowen, Philip Nichols Jr., Marion T. Bennett. Washington: [U.S. Superintendent of Documents], 1978.
    The first of these volumes is devoted to judicial biography, while the second is a substantial account of the development of the court itself.

United States Tax Court Practice and Procedure. Lester M. Ponder. Englewood Cliffs: Prentice Hall, 1976.
    An account of the background, jurisdiction, and procedures appropriate to the Tax Court.

The Court of Private Land Claims: The Adjudication of Spanish and Mexican Land Grant Titles, 1891-1904. Richard Wells Bradfute. Albuquerque: University of New Mexico Press, 1975.

This is the story of the special court created to handle cases involving Spanish and Mexican land grant titles, 1891–1901. There is a useful bibliography.

MILITARY JUSTICE

Miliatry justice stands apart from the main streams of administrative law and regular jurisprudence, yet in principle it can be viewed as a species of administrative law. The works listed below will introduce this often controversial area.

Military Justice in the Armed Forces of the United States. Robinson O. Everett. Harrisburg, Pa.: Military Service Publishing Co., 1956. (Reprinted by Greenwood Press, 1976).

Considers a variety of military legal procedures including the various kinds of courts-martial and appellate review. There is a full chapter on the United States Court of Military Appeals.

Justice Under Fire: A Study of Military Law. Joseph W. Bishop, Jr. New York: Charterhouse, 1974.

A well executed attempt to look at military justice. It treats of background, courts-martial system and jurisdiction, application of the Bill of Rights to service personnel, various aspects of the application of military powers, and the laws of war.

Military Law and Military Justice. 3rd Revision. [U.S. Court of Military Appeals, Library]. [Washington]: Librarian; U.S. Court of Military Appeals, 1972.

A large bibliography of materials pertinent to military justice both U.S. and foreign.

Military Justice is to Justice as Military Music is to Music. Robert Sherrill. New York: Harper & Row, 1970.

Simply put, this is a highly critical account of military justice complete with specific instances and gory details.

Manual for Courts-Martial United States. Rev. ed. Washington: U.S. Government Printing Office, 1969.

This manual and addenda set forth the courts-martial procedures for the armed forces as recharted after World War II.

COMPARATIVE ADMINISTRATIVE LAW

Comparative administrative legal materials present a fascinating complement to the traditional American pattern of development. This section points to a few leading sources, mostly in English, for administrative law in other societies. It has considerable value for purposes of intellectual cross-fertilization. Many of these works contain useful bibliographies. For other works and some in foreign languages, see the Selected Bibliography (chapter 7) at the end of this book.

Administrative Law. 5th ed. H. W. R. Wade. Oxford: Clarendon Press, 1982.
    A leading contemporary survey of British administrative law.

Cases and Materials on Administrative Law in Nigeria. B.O. Iluyomade and B.U. Eka. Ile-Ife, Nigeria: University of Ife Press, 1980.
    The only volume on Nigerian administrative law. Cases predominate.

Traite de droit administratif. 2 vols. André de Laubadère. 8th ed. Paris: Librairie generale de droit et de jurisprudence, 1980.
    A leading comprehensive treatise on French administrative law, it studies the subject at the university level.

Comparative Constitutional and Administrative Law. Alan Holoch, Jill Mubarak. Los Angeles: University of Southern California Law Center, 1979.
    This little volume is a very useful bibliography.

Legal Control of Government: Administrative Law in Britain and the United States. Bernard Schwartz and H. W. R. Wade. Oxford: Clarendon Press, 1972.
    An up-to-date treatment by two leading scholars of comparative administrative law, considering British and American experience.

The Administrative Functions of the French Conseil d'Etat. Margherita Rendel. London: London School of Economics and Political Science, 1970.
    A study of the French supreme court for administrative law with emphasis on its administrative role.

Le controle judiciare de l'administration au Quebec. Rene Dussault. Quebec: Les presses de l'Universite-Laval, 1969.
    A study of administrative law in Quebec.

Judicial Control of Administrative Action in India and Pakistan. M. A. Fazal. Oxford: Clarendon Press, 1969.
    A study of administrative law principles and remedies as developed in the Indian subcontinent.

Die Entstehung des Verwaltungsrechts als Rechtsdisziplin. Hans-Joachim Feist. Munchen: Verlag UNI-Druck, 1968.
    This little volume is a brief introduction to the origins of administrative law as a legal course of study in Germany.

French Administrative Law. L. Neville Brown, J. F. Garner, and Nicole Questiaux. London: Butterworths, 1967.

A brief discussion of French administrative law as an exercise in comparative law for the British student.

Ombudsmen and Other Citizen's Protectors in Nine Countries. Walter Gellhorn. Cambridge: Harvard University Press, 1966.
   A leading U.S. study of the ombudsman's office.

The Censorial System of Ming China. Charles O. Hucker. Stanford: Stanford University Press, 1966.
   Professor Hucker's work is the only full length treatment of the Chinese Censorate and is particularly useful as an example of a pertinent East Asian procedure drawn from another era.

The Ombudsman: Citizen's Defender, 2d ed. Donald C. Rowat, ed. London: George Allen & Unwin Ltd., 1968.
   This volume details the development of the ombudsman in Sweden as well as comparable entities elsewhere in Scandanavia. In addition, it has materials on related institutions in a number of other countries.

Soviet Administrative Legality. Glenn G. Morgan. Stanford: Stanford University Press, 1962.
   A study of the supervisory role of the Russian attorney general's office. It has decided administrative law overtones.

An Outline of Administrative and Local Government Law in Scotland. J. Bennett Miller. Edinburgh: W. Green & Son Ltd., 1961.
   A useful study of a specialized aspect of British (Scottish) administrative law.

Derecho administrativo. 2d ed. Andres Serra Rojas. Mexico, D.F.: Libreria de Manuel Parrua, 1961.
   A massive work on the Mexican administrative and constitutional system with emphasis on administrative law. It contains a lengthy international bibliography.

O Controle dos atos administrativos pelo poder judiciario. Terceiro edicao. M. Seaba Fegundes. Rio de Janeiro: Edino Revista Forense, 1957.
   A lengthy Brazilian study of administrative law.

Allgemeines Verwaltungsrecht. Bernd Bender. Freiburg: Verlag Eberhard Albert, 1956.
   A short work on general administrative law in Germany.

French Administrative Law and the Common-Law World. Bernard Schwartz. New York: New York University Press, 1954.

This is the best known comparison of French and Anglican administrative law written in English. In addition to substantive material it contains a brief but very helpful reference section.

The Judicial Control of Public Authorities in England and Italy. Sergio Galeotti. London: Stevens and Sons, Ltd., 1954.
   The principal work in English on Italian administrative law. Its comparative treatment in conjunction with British usage makes it particularly valuable. There is a useful bibliography, too.

Administration of Justice in Latin America. Helen C. Clagett. New York: Oceana Publications, 1952.
   Chapter 4 of this work includes information on the administrative courts in Latin America. It also has a useful bibliography.

Justice and Administrative Law: A Study of the British Constitution. 3d ed. William A. Robson. London: Stevens & Sons, 1951. (Reprint by Greenwood Press, 1970).
   A major treatise on British administrative law, it includes a summary of the British administrative tribunals.

Law in the Modern State. Leon Duguit. New York: B. W. Huebsch, 1919.
   A translation by Frida and Harold Laski of Duguit's *Transformations du droit public*, a now classic theoretical statement about the nature of law. It contains chapters, more narrow in point, on administrative acts and administrative law.

Comparative Administrative Law. [two vols. in one] Frank J. Goodnow. New York: G. P. Putnam's Sons, 1893.
   This classic work considers the administrative systems and pertinent law of the United States, England, France, and Germany as of 1893.

INTERNATIONAL ADMINISTRATIVE LAW

The materials available for the study of the international aspects of administrative law are scarce. Some of those listed here are concerned with resolution of legal issues pertaining to employees. Others have to do with limited authority to promulgate rules.

International Regulatory Regimes. 2 vols. David M. Leive. Lexington, Mass.: Lexington Books, D.C. Heath, 1976.
   This two-volume work concentrates on rule-making in three international agency settings: the World Health Organization, the World Meterological Organization, and the Joint Food Standards program.

The United Nations Administrative Tribunal. Byung Chul Koh. Baton Rouge: Lousiana State University Press, 1966.

A principal but brief study of UN administrative legal procedures. It contains a useful bibliography.

Interpretation of Ambiguous Documents by International Administrative Tribunals. A. H. Schechter. New York: Praeger, 1964.

Schechter's little volume compares the three main international administrative law tribunals.

The Proper Law of International Organizations. C. Wilfred Jenks. London: Stevens & Sons Ltd., and Dobbs Ferry, N.Y.: Oceana Publications, 1962.

Includes material on administrative law emanating from international agencies.

International Tribunals: Past and Future. Manley O. Hudson. New York: Carnegie Endowment for International Peace, 1944.

Centers primarily on the more prominent international courts, but it has useful information on the background of international administrative tribunals.

OUTLINE SERIES

The four works listed in this section are particularly useful as study guides for law students and as review for the bar examinations. They are comparable to traditional academic outline texts, but they cannot ordinarily be used in lieu of more substantial texts, casebooks, and other sources; and, if outdated, can be downright misleading. In the following they are not separately annotated.

Administrative Law and Process in a Nutshell. Ernest Gellhorn, Barry B. Boyer. St. Paul: West Publishing Co., 1981.

Administrative Law. 8th ed. Michael R. Asimov. Gardena, Calif.: Gilbert Law Summaries, 1981.

Outline of Administrative Law. William T. Miller and Grace Powers Monaco. Irvington-on-Hudson, N.Y.: Blackstone Law Summaries, 1975.

Smith's Review Legal Gem Series: Administrative Law. 2d ed. Myron G. Hill, Jr., Howard Rossen, Wilton S. Sogg. St. Paul: West Publishing Co., 1977.

TEXTS ON PUBLIC ADMINISTRATION
CONTAINING SECTIONS ON ADMINISTRATIVE LAW

Not all texts in public administration include consideration of administrative law, but the following are among the significant sources that do. They are not individually annotated.

The Craft of Public Administration. 3d ed. George E. Berkley. Boston: Allyn and Bacon, Inc., 1981. Chapter 11, pp. 382–423.

Dynamics of Public Bureaucracy: An Introduction to Public Management. 2d ed. Fred A. Kramer. Cambridge: Winthrop Publishers, 1981. Chapter 12, pp. 378–397.

Contemporary Public Administration. Thomas Vocino and Jack Rabin. New York: Harcourt Brace Jovanovich, Inc., 1981. Chapter 7 (by Victor G. Rosenblum), pp. 145–175.

American Public Administration: Concepts and Cases. 2d ed. Carl E. Lutrin and Allen K. Settle. Palo Alto, Calif.: Mayfield Publishing Co., 1980. Chapter 8, pp. 270–293.

Modern Public Administration. 5th ed. Felix A. and Lloyd G. Nigro. New York: Harper & Row, 1980. Chapter 20, pp. 453–71.

Public Administration. Robert S. Lorch. St. Paul: West Publishing Co., 1978. Chapter 14, pp. 283–298.

Public Administration: A Critical Perspective. Robert D. Miewald. New York: McGraw Hill, 1978. Chapter 11, pp. 236–57.

Public Administration: Values, Policy, and Change. Robert H. Simmons and Eugene P. Dvorin. New York: Alfred Publishing Co., 1977. Chapter 8, pp. 257–286.

Public Administration: Government in Action. Ivan L. Richardson and Sidney Baldwin. Columbus, Ohio: Charles E. Merrill Publishing Co., 1976. Chapter 7, pp. 105–118.

Public Administration. 5th ed. John M. Pfiffner and Robert Presthus. New York: Ronald Press, 1967. Part VI, Chapters 25–28, pp. 425–506. (The 6th ed. by Presthus contains only chapter 20, pp. 391–409).

Public Administration and Policy: Selected Essays. Peter Woll, ed. New York: Harper Torchbooks, 1966. Unit 5, pp. 190–220.

Public Administration. Revised ed. Marshall Edward Dimock, Gladys Ogden Dimock, and Louis W. Koenig. New York: Rinehart & Co., 1960. Chapter 29, pp. 503–522.

Government and Public Administration: The Quest for Responsible Performance.
John D. Millett. New York: McGraw-Hill Book Co., 1959. Chapters 21–24 deal
with administrative law.

Introduction to the Study of Public Administration. 4th ed. Leonard D. White.
New York: MacMillan, 1955. Chapter 31–34, pp. 463–521.

Elements of Public Administration. Fritz Morstein Marx, ed. New York: Prentice
Hall Inc., 1946. Chapter 23 (by Don K. Price) pp. 519–543.

5

Citations: Footnote and Bibliographical Entries

Writing a paper for a course in administrative law carries with it the same responsibility as a paper for any other college level course. Footnotes are designed to convey both credit and blame for facts and ideas that are not the result of the writer's own research. Few facts and ideas are truly original. Moreover, for law related research papers it is often appropriate to cite original government agency or court materials. Therefore, the typical administrative law paper will tend to contain a greater number of footnotes than a paper written, say, for an organization theory course.

WHAT TO FOOTNOTE

Footnotes that refer to quotations, facts, and explanatory or discursive materials should be present in any Ph.D. dissertation, master's thesis, honors paper, or term paper that fulfills a major portion of the requirements for a course or degree. Because most administrative law research papers consist mainly of scholarly research from primary sources (e.g., court and agency decisions, rules and regulations), extensive numbers of citations are usually present. Yet not all quotations, facts, and ideas need to be referenced. To overdocument or underdocument research is to err. Here is a brief statement of when footnotes are appropriate.

Quotations

Except those of common knowledge, quotations should be footnoted. For example, references to particular sentences in a judge's opinion or a statutory provision are frequently cited in administrative law papers. It is generally regarded as poor form though to quote extensively from judicial opinions or statutes unless the statements are regarded by the writer to be of such significance and character that the point being made could not be conveyed adequately otherwise. A skillful writer will paraphrase direct quotations whenever possible, retaining only those sentences or phrases which are particularly compelling. Of course, the paraphrased materials must be cited just as a direct quotation and such paraphrasing must reflect accurately the meaning of the original passage.

Facts

All facts, except those that are part of common knowledge, must be footnoted. Consider whether the average reader is likely to be aware of the origin and authenticity of the facts. If in doubt, footnote it.

There are three criteria for footnoting facts.[1] First, all facts over which honest persons may disagree, which is to say, *controversial* facts, should be cited. Second, if a significant part of the writer's argument rests on the truth or falsity of the statement in question, then it, too, should be cited as a footnote. And last, whenever the fact in question is obscure—that is, the means by which the fact may be established as authentic is beyond the average reader's experience or recall— it must be cited.

Explanatory Remarks

Writers of law related papers often indulge in the use of footnotes to explain or elaborate a point made in the body of the text. For example, following a discussion of a court's majority opinion contained in the body of the text the substance of the court's minority opinion may be placed in a footnote. The curious reader is thus apprised of the minority view without unduly distracting the average reader's attention from the substance of the point being made in the body of the text.

Providing this additional information is only one legitimate use for explanatory footnotes. Writers will employ such footnotes to provide background on research methodology, to trace the origin of an idea, to comment on the importance of any source as well as for other uses.[2] The employment of explanatory footnotes can add greatly to the intellectual depth exhibited in a paper and will reflect the author's understanding of the subtleties of the subject matter.

BIBLIOGRAPHY

A bibliography is a listing of every relevant work examined in writing the paper. It should include all works cited in the footnotes plus any other works which were examined and in the considered judgment of the writer relevant to the topic.

---

1. Albert P. Melone and Carl Kalvelage, *Primer on Constitutional Law* (Pacific Palisades, Calif.: Palisades Publishers, 1982), p. 50.
2. Morley Segal, Albert P. Melone, and Carl Kalvelage, *Political Science: Thinking, Researching, and Writing About the Discipline* (Pacific Palisades, Calif.: Palisades Publishers, 1983).

The purpose of a bibliography is twofold. First, it indicates at a glance which sources were employed and might be of value for further study. Second, it provides a tool to ascertain whether the writer employed all relevant and available materials. Instructors will often begin their evaluation of a term paper by considering the quality and quantity of the bibliographical entries.

Sources should normally be placed in mutually exclusive categories. That is, if the bibliographical entries are at all numerous and sufficiently differentiated, then breaking down the entry presentation into source categories is useful. Some idea of the numerous possible categories may be glimpsed by turning to the section of this chapter that contains sample footnotes and bibliography. Obviously, the number of categories needed will vary with the total number of bibliographical entries. However, it is always advisable to separate court opinions from the other references under the title, *Cases*. For the typical administrative law paper, divide the entries into the following categories: Books, Journals or Magazine Articles, Legal Periodicals, Government Documents, Statutory Materials, and Cases (including law court and administrative agency decisions). Treat this suggestion as a guide, not as the last word. The instructor is always the last word in such matters.

FORM

Footnote and bibliography forms are among the few things in life about which one can justifiably be arbitrary. There is no inherent reason to use one form rather than another, so long as the communication is clear and consistent. The works used should be cited in the same form as in indexes, bibliographies, and library catalogs. In this way, a reader will be able to locate cited sources.

What follows are examples of the most frequent types of footnotes and bibliographic entries used in a political science paper. Most of the forms are based upon: *The Chicago Manual of Style*, 13th ed., rev. (Chicago: University of Chicago Press, 1982); Kate L. Turabian, *A Manual for Writers of Term Papers, Theses and Dissertations*, 4th ed. (Chicago: University of Chicago Press, 1973); and *A Uniform System of Citation*, 13th ed. (Cambridge: Harvard Law Review Association, 1981). The last source was employed only for materials subsumed under the legal citation section on pages 92–95. Although the forms presented probably meet the requirements of most instructors, there is an alternative form of citation gaining prominence within political science circles. The scientific reference format follows the examples for the more conventional forms of footnote and bibliographical citation.

Footnotes, General Rules

Books should include:
1. Author's full name (as it appears in the book)
2. Complete title

   3. Editor, compiler, or translator (if any)
   4. Name of series, volume or series number (if any)
   5. Number of volumes
   6. City, publisher, and date
   7. Volume number and page number

Articles should include:
   1. Author
   2. Title of article
   3. Periodical
   4. Date and page numbers of article

Unpublished material should include:
   1. Author
   2. Title (if any)
   3. Type of material
   4. Where it may be found
   5. Date
   6. Page number (if any)

Bibliography, General Rules

Footnote style can be changed into bibliographic style by transposing the author's first and last names, removing parentheses from facts of publication, omitting page references, and repunctuating with periods instead of commas. Books should include:
   1. Name of author(s), editors, or responsible institutions
   2. Full title, including subtitle if one exists
   3. Series (if any)
   4. Volume number
   5. Edition, if not the original
   6. Location and name of publisher (sometimes omitted)
   7. Date of publication

Articles should include:
   1. Name of author
   2. Title of article
   3. Name of periodical
   4. Volume and number (or date, or both)
   5. Pages

BOOKS

Book With One Author

Footnote: 1.   Kenneth F. Warren, *Administrative Law In the American Political System* (St. Paul: West Publishing Co., 1982), p. 22.

Bibliography: Warren, Kenneth F. *Administrative Law In the American Political System*. St. Paul: West Publishing Co., 1982.

Book With Two Authors

Footnote: 2.   Donald D. Barry and Howard R. Whitcomb, *The Legal Foundations of Public Administration* (St. Paul: West Publishing Co.,
1981), p. 27.

Bibliography: Barry, Donald D. and Whitcomb, Howard R. *The Legal Foundations of Public Administration*. St. Paul: West Publishing Co.,
1981.

Book With Three Authors

Footnote: 3.   Walter Gellhorn, Clark Byse, and Peter L. Strauss, *Administrative
Law: Cases and Comments*, 7th ed. (Mineola, N.Y.: The Founda-
tion Press, Inc., 1979), p. 235.

Bibliography: Gellhorn, Walter; Byse, Clark; and Strauss, Peter L. *Administrative Law: Cases and Comments*. 7th ed. Mineola, N.Y.:
The Foundation Press, Inc., 1979.

Book With More Than Three Authors

Footnote: 4.   Neil A. Kaplan, et al., *Parallel Grand Jury and Administrative
Agency Investigations* (Chicago: American Bar Association/Pro-
fessional Education Publications, 1981), p. 10.

Bibliography: Kaplan, Neil A.; Friedman, Paul L.; Bennett, Robert S.; and
Trainor, Helen C. *Parallel Grand Jury and Administrative Agen-
cy Investigations*. Chicago: American Bar Association/Professional
Education Publications, 1981.

Edition of a Book Other Than First

Footnote: 5.   Gerald E. Caiden, *Public Administration*, 2d ed. (Pacific Palisades,
Calif.: Palisades Publishers, 1982), p. 283.

Bibliography: Caiden, Gerald E. *Public Administration*. 2d ed. Pacific Palisades,
Calif.: Palisades Publishers, 1982.

Book in a Series

Footnote: 6.   Ernest Gellhorn, *Antitrust Law and Economics*, West Nutshell
Series (St. Paul: West Publishing Co., 1977), p. 392.

Bibliography: Gellhorn, Ernest. *Antitrust Law and Economics*. West Nutshell
Series. St. Paul: West Publishing Co., 1977.

Book By Editor Or Translator

Footnote: 7.   Dwight Waldo, ed., *Public Administration in a Time of Tur-
bulence* (Scranton, Pa.: Chandler Publishing Co., 1971), pp.
274–276.

Bibliography: Waldo, Dwight, ed. *Public Administration in a Time Of Tur-
bulence*. Scranton, Pa.: Chandler Publishing Co., 1971.

Translators
Footnote: 8.   Leon Duguit, *Law in the Modern State*, trans. Frida and Harold
                 Laski (New York: B. W. Huebsch, 1919), p. 164.
Bibliography: Duguit, Leon. *Law in the Modern State*. Translated by Frida and
                 Harold Laski. New York: B. W. Huebsch, 1919.
Comment: When the author and translator names both appear on the title
                 page, the translator's name should be located after the title.
                 However, if the author's name is not on the title page the
                 translator's name should appear first, followed by the word, trans.

Book, Multivolume
Footnote: 9.   Kenneth Culp Davis, *Administrative Law Treatise*, 2d ed., 3 vols.
                 (San Diego: K. C. Davis, University of San Diego, 1978), 1:225.
Bibliography: Davis, Kenneth Culp. *Administrative Law Treatise*, 2d ed. Vol.
                 1. San Diego: K. C. Davis, University of San Diego, 1978.

Citation in One Book from Another Book
Footnote: 10.   K. C. Davis, 1 *Administrative Law Treatise*, pp. 2–3. As cited in
                 Donald D. Barry and Howard R. Whitcomb, *The Legal Founda-
                 tions of Public Administration* (St. Paul: West Publishing Co.,
                 1981), p. 2.
Bibliography: Barry, Donald D. and Whitcomb, Howard R. *The Legal Founda-
                 tions of Public Administration*. St. Paul: West Publishing Co.,
                 1981.

Book Review
Footnote: 11.   Richard Dale, Review of *Apartheid and International Organiza-
                 tions* by Richard E. Bissell, *The Annals of the American Academy
                 of Political and Social Science* 44 (November, 1978): 178.
Bibliography: Dale, Richard. Review of *Apartheid and International Organiza-
                 tions* by Richard E. Bissell. *The Annals of the American Academy
                 of Political and Social Science* 44 (November, 1978): 177–179.
Comment: The first name cited is that of the reviewer of the book. The second
                 name cited is the author of the book.

Book In a Series, One Author, Several Volumes, Each With a Different Title
Footnote: 12.   Arthur M. Schlesinger, *The Age of Roosevelt*, 3 vols., *The Politics
                 of Upheaval* (Boston: Houghton Mifflin, 1960), 3:174.
Bibliography: Schlesinger, Arthur M. *The Age of Roosevelt*. Vol. 3. *The Politics
                 of Upheaval*. Boston: Houghton Mifflin, 1960.

Paperback Edition of Book First Published in Hard Cover
Footnote: 13.   Theodore J. Lowi, *The End of Liberalism: The Second Republic of
                 the United States*, 2d ed. (New York: W. W. Norton and Co.,
                 paperback, 1979), pp. 56–59.

Bibliography: Lowi, Theodore J. *The End of Liberalism: The Second Republic of the United States.* 2d ed. Paperback. New York: W. W. Norton and Co., 1979.

Introduction or Foreword to Book by Another Author
Footnote: 14. Harold J. Laski, Introduction to *Law in the Modern State* by Leon Duguit, trans. Frida and Harold Laski (New York: B. W. Huebsch, 1919), p. xii.
Bibliography: Laski, Harold J. Introduction to *Law in the Modern State.* By Leon Duguit, translated by Frida and Harold Laski. New York: B. W. Huebsch, 1919.
Comment: The first appearing name is the person writing the foreword or introduction to the book. It is his or her comments which are being footnoted, not those of the author of the book.

Book With an Association as Author
Footnote: 15. American Bar Association Special Constitutional Convention Study Committee, *Amendment of the Constitution By the Convention Method Under Article V* (Chicago: American Bar Association, 1974), p. 36.
Bibliography: American Bar Association Special Constitutional Convention Study Committee. *Amendment of the Constitution By the Convention Method Under Article V.* Chicago: American Bar Association, 1974.

Author's Name Not on Title Page, but Known
Footnote: 16. [Alexander Hamilton, James Madison, and John Jay], *The Federalist* (New York: The Modern Library, 1941), p. 129.
Bibliography: [Hamilton, Alexander; Madison, James; and Jay, John.] *The Federalist.* New York: The Modern Library, 1941.

Article, Chapter, or Other Part of a Book
Footnote: 17. Leandro A. Viloria, "The Presidential Complaints and Action Commitee in the Philippines," *The Ombudsman: Citizen's Defender*, 2d ed., edited by Donald C. Rowat (London: George Allen & Unwin Ltd., 1968), p. 153.
Bibliography: Rowat, Donald C., ed. *The Ombudsman: Citizen's Defender*, 2d ed. London: George Allen & Unwin Ltd., 1968.

JOURNAL OR MAGAZINE ARTICLES

Periodical: Author Given [Non-Legal]
Footnote: 18. Harry Guenther, "Deregulation—Is It Happening in Banking?" *Regulation: AEI Journal on Government and Society* 4 (Nov./Dec., 1980): 42.

Bibliography: Guenther, Harry. "Deregulation—Is It Happening in Banking?" *Regulation: AEI Journal on Government and Society* 4 (Nov./Dec., 1980): 42–49.

Comment: See footnote #68 at page 95 for recommended citation form for legal periodicals.

Magazine Article, No Author Given
Footnote: 19. "Making Museums Modest," *Newsweek*, 26 July 1982, p. 66.
Bibliography: "Making Museums Modest." *Newsweek*, 26 July 1982, p. 66.

Magazine Article, Author Given
Footnote: 20. Hugh Sidey, "A Flash of Irish Flint," *Time*, October 18, 1982, p. 25.
Bibliography: Sidey, Hugh, "A Flash of Irish Flint." *Time*, October 18, 1982, p. 25.

NEWSPAPERS

Footnote: 21. "U.S. Court Denies Bid for Agent Orange Data," *The New York Times*, 26 July 1982, p. 7.
Bibliography: "U.S. Court Denies Bid for Agent Orange Data." *The New York Times*, 26 July, 1982, p. 7.
Comment: When author byline is presented, name author at beginning of citation. For foreign newspapers in which the city is not part of the title, place the city name in parentheses, e.g., *Le Monde* (Paris).

ENCYCLOPEDIAS, ALMANACS, AND OTHER REFERENCE WORKS EXCLUDING LEGAL MATERIALS

Signed Articles
Footnote: 22. *International Encyclopedia of the Social Sciences*, 5th ed., s.v. "Administrative Law," by Bernard Schwartz.
Bibliography: *International Encyclopedia of the Social Sciences*, 5th ed. s.v. "Administrative Law," by Bernard Schwartz.

Unsigned Articles
Footnote: 23. *The World Almanac and Book of Facts 1982*, s.v. "Consumer Survival Kit—Social Security Programs: After the Paychecks Stop."
Bibliography: *The World Almanac and Book of Facts 1982*. s.v. "Consumer Survival Kit—Social Security Programs: After the Paychecks Stop."
Comment: When citing this type of reference work the place of publication, publisher, date, and page numbers are normally omitted. However, editions other than the first should be specified. The letters s.v. mean sub verbo, "under the word;" i.e., under the designated title.

Material from Manuscript Collections
Footnote: 24. Administration of Justice and Courts, 1916–, Richard Richards papers, Library of University of California, Los Angeles, California, p. 5.
Bibliography: Los Angeles, California. Library of University of California, Los Angeles, Administration of Justice and Courts, 1916–. Richard Richards Papers.

Radio and Television Programs
Footnote: 25. NBC, *NBC NIGHTLY NEWS*, 5 December 1979, "Iranian Crisis," Hilary Brown, reporter.
Bibliography: NBC. NBC NIGHTLY NEWS. 5 December 1979. "Iranian Crisis." Hilary Brown, reporter.

Interviews
Footnote: 26. Interview with Anne M. Gorsuch, Commissioner, Environmental Protection Agency, Washington, D.C., October 26, 1981.
Bibliography: Gorsuch, Anne M. Commissioner, Environmental Protection Agency. Washington, D.C. Interview, 26 October 1981.

Letters
Footnote: 27. Lawrence to Barr, 8 November 1958, Political Papers of Governor David Leo Lawrence, Hillman Library, University of Pittsburgh, Pittsburgh, Pa.
Bibliography: Pittsburgh, Pa. Hillman Library, University of Pittsburgh. Political Papers of Governor David Leo Lawrence. Lawrence to Barr, 8 November 1958.

Mimeographed or Other Nonprinted Reports
Footnote: 28. Donald C. Stone, "The Response of Higher Education to the Administrative Needs of the Public Service," mimeographed (The National Association of Schools of Public Affairs and Administration), April, 1971, p. 17.
Bibliography: Stone, Donald C. "The Response of Higher Education to the Administrative Needs of the Public Service." The National Association of Schools of Public Affairs and Administration, April, 1971.

Pamphlets
Footnote: 29. Herman Mertins, Jr., ed., *Professional Standards and Ethics: A Workbook for Public Administrators* (Washington, D.C.: American Society for Public Administration, 1979), p. 17.
Bibliography: Mertins, Herman Jr., ed. *Professional Standards and Ethics: A Workbook for Public Administrators*. Washington, D.C.: American Society for Public Administration, 1979.

Proceedings of a Meeting or Conference: Reproduced

Footnote: 30. Annual Report of the American Bar Association Including Proceedings of the Ninety-Ninth Annual Meeting, "Report No. 1 of
the Section of Administrative Law," (Atlanta, Ga.: August 9–12,
1976), p. 968.

Bibliography: Annual Report of the American Bar Association Including Proceedings of the Ninety-Ninth Annual Meeting, "Report No. 1 of
the Section of Administrative Law." Atlanta, Ga.: August 9–12,
1976.

Paper Read or Speech Delivered at a Meeting

Footnote: 31. Robert T. Daland, "Bureaucracy in Brazil: Attitudes of Civilian
Top Executives Toward Change" (Paper delivered at the 1971
Meetings of the National Conference on Comparative Administra-
tion), Syracuse, N.Y., April, 1971, p. 7.

Bibliography: Daland, Robert T. "Bureacracy in Brazil: Attitudes of Civilian Top
Executives Toward Change." Paper delivered at the 1971 Meetings
of the National Conference on Comparative Administration,
April, 1971, at Syracuse, N.Y.

Thesis or Dissertation

Footnote: 32. Michael Vasu, "Politics and Planning: A National Study of the
American Institute of Planners" (Ph.D. Dissertation, Southern
Illinois University, Carbondale, 1976), p. 195.

Bibliography: Vasu, Michael. "Politics and Planning: A National Study of the
American Institute of Planners." Ph.D. Dissertation, Southern Illinois University, Carbondale, 1976.

GOVERNMENT DOCUMENTS

Because the form is totally unlike that of books and magazines proper government document citation is a difficult problem. The card catalog is a good guide,
and the following general rules should help. Include in this order the following:

1. The country or jurisdiction (e.g., U.S., Ill.)

2. The branch of government (legislative, executive, judicial)

3. The subbranch or subbranches of government (e.g., House, Committee on
Education and Labor).

Determining the branches or subbranches is not always immediately apparent.
However, a careful examination of the document itself, its entry in the card catalog,
or the *Government Organization Manual* should give an idea as to the sequence
of organization.

This information is followed by the title (underlined), the name of the series
or sequence, and the facts of publication, meaning the place of publication, the
publisher, and the date of publication. The following examples include some of

the most commonly cited government publications students of administrative law are likely to encounter.

Congressional Documents

Bills

Footnote: 33. U.S., Congress, House, *Federal Water Pollution Control Act*, H.R. 4503, 97th Cong., 1st sess., 1981, p. 1.
Bibliography: U.S. Congress. House. *Federal Water Pollution Control Act*. H.R. 4503, 97th Cong., 1st sess., 1981.

Footnote: 34. U.S. Congress, Senate, *Freedom of Information Act*, S. 1730, 97th Cong., 2nd sess., 1982, p. 3.
Bibliography: U.S. Congress. Senate. *Freedom of Information Act*. S. 1730, 97th Cong., 2nd sess., 1982.

Debates

Footnote: 35. U.S. Congress, Senate, The 1983 Budget Resolution: The Factor of Forty-Four, and Other Depressing Thoughts, 97th Cong., 2nd sess., 19 May 1982, *Congressional Record*, 128, no. 61: S 5457.
Bibliography: U.S. Congress. Senate. The 1983 Budget Resolution: The Factor of Forty-Four, and Other Depressing Thoughts. 97th Cong., 2nd sess., 19 May 1982. *Congressional Record*, vol. 128, no. 61.

Reports

Footnote: 36. U.S. Congress, Senate, *Criminal Code Reform Act of 1981*, S. Rept. 97–307 to accompany S. 1630, 97th Cong., 1st sess., 1981.
Bibliography: U.S. Congress. Senate. *Criminal Code Reform Act of 1981*. S. Rept. 97–307 to accompany S. 1630. 97th Cong., 1st sess. 1981.

Hearings

Footnote: 37. U.S., Congress, Senate, Committee on Finance, *Trade Agreements Act of 1979, S. 1376, Hearings before the Subcommittee on International Trade of the Senate Committee on Finance on S. 1376*, 96th Cong., 1st sess., 1979, pp. 393–396.
Bibliography: U.S. Congress. Senate. Committee on Finance. *Trade Agreements Act of 1979, S. 1376. Hearings Before the Subcommittee on International Trade of the Senate Committee on Finance on S. 1376*. 96th Cong., 1st sess., 1979.

Executive Documents

From an Executive Department

Footnote: 38. U.S., Department of Energy, Economic Regulatory Administration, Office of Fuels Programs, *Draft Environmental Impact Statement: Conversion to Coal, Consolidated Edison Arthur Kill*

Generating Station, Boilers 20 and 30, New York City, Staten Island, New York (Springfield, Virginia: National Technical Information Service, 1982), pp. 4–11.

Bibliography: U.S. Department of Energy. Economic Regulatory Administration. Office of Fuels Programs. *Draft Environmental Impact Statement; Conversion to Coal, Consolidated Edison Arthur Kill Generating Station, Boilers 20 and 30, New York City, Staten Island, New York.* Springfield, Virginia: National Technical Information Service, 1982.

Footnote: 39. U.S., Department of State, *Annual Report of the Inspector General of the Department of State and Foreign Service*, Department of Foreign Service Series 305, Department of State Publication 9267 (May 1982), pp. 6–9.

Bibliography: U.S. Department of State. *Annual Report of the Inspector General of the Department of State and Foreign Service.* Department of Foreign Service Series 305, Department of State Publication 9267 (May 1982).

Comment: Many executive department documents carry a publication number and or a publication series number. It is a good idea to include such information in citations. Also, some executive documents will contain author names. Although it is permissible to cite author names it is not always practical; libraries often catalog the name of the sponsoring government agency and not author names.

Presidential Papers

Footnote: 40. U.S. President, 'Remarks and a Question-and-Answer Session at a Briefing for State and Local Officials, July 6, 1982," *Weekly Compilation of Presidential Documents*, vol. 18, no. 27, July 12, 1982, pp. 876–77.

Bibliography: U.S. President. "Remarks and a Question-and-Answer Session at a Briefing for State and Local Officials, July 6, 1982." *Weekly Compilation of Presidential Documents.* July 12, 1982.

INTERNATIONAL DOCUMENTS

International Organizations

Footnote: 41. United Nations, Department of International Economic and Social Affairs, *1979 Yearbook of International Trade Statistics*, vol. 2 (ST/ESA/STAT/SER.G/28/Add. 1), 1980, p. 295.

Bibliography: United Nations. Department of International Economic and Social Affairs. *1979 Yearbook of International Trade Statistics.* Vol. 2 (ST/ESA/STAT/SER.G/28/Add.1), 1980.

Comment: Turabian suggests that the following elements be presented for each international document citation: authorizing body, paper topic, document or series number if available, and date.

Treaties

Footnote: 42. U.S., *Statutes at Large*, vol. 59, pt. 2 (1945), "Surrender of Japan," 2 September 1945.
Bibliography: U.S. Statutes at Large, vol. 59, pt. 2(1945). "Surrender of Japan," 2 September 1945.

Footnote: 43. U.S., Department of State, *United States Treaties and Other International Agreements*, vol. 31, pt. 1, "Japan-Extradition," TIAS No. 9625, 3 March 1978.
Bibiography: U.S. Department of State. *United States Treaties and Other International Agreements*, vol. 31, pt. 1. "Japan-Extradition," TIAS No. 9625, 3 March 1978.
Comment: Since 1950, U.S. Treaties may be found in *United States Treaties and Other International Agreements*. The United Nations and its predecessor, League of Nations, have treaty series which are additional sources for treaties and international agreements.

STATE AND LOCAL DOCUMENTS

State

Footnote: 44. Illinois, Secretary of State, *Handbook of Illinois Government*, June 1981, p. 99.
Bibliography: Illinois. Secretary of State. *Handbook of Illinois Government*. June 1981.

Footnote: 45. Illinois, *Constitution*, art, 8, sec. 3.
Bibliography: Illinois. *Constitution*.
Comment: Provide the date of the constitution if the constitution cited is not one currently in force, e.g., Illinois, *Constitution* (1848), art. 1, sec. 2.

Local

Footnote: 46. Carbondale, Illinois, City Manager, "City of Carbondale, Illinois Annual Budget FY 1979–80," mimeographed (April 9, 1979), pp. 23–27.
Bibliography: Carbondale, Illinois. City Manager. "City of Carbondale, Illinois Annual Budget FY 1979–80." April 9, 1979.
Comment: In general, citations for state and local government documents should follow the form for U.S. federal documents. Researchers

will often encounter insufficient documentation for state and local materials. Improvise when necessary since many of these materials are not cataloged.

LEGAL CITATIONS

The forms for the legal citations that follow are consistent with those recommended in *A Uniform System of Citation*, 13th ed. (Cambridge: Harvard Law Review Association, 1981). The Harvard Blue Book, as it is often called, provides a guide to citations appropriate for works predominately legal, written for a professional legal audience. Because typical users of this book are most likely to be social science students or public administration practitioners (not legal professionals), *A Uniform System of Citation* for all entries has not been used. Rather, the Blue Book for legal, qua legal, materials only, has been followed. This decision, however, creates a slight problem. *A Uniform System of Citation* provides guidance for footnote, not bibliographical entries; in fact, it makes no distinction between the two. Some works transform legal footnote entries into bibliographical entries consistent with the rules found on page 82 of this book.[3] After consulting expert opinion and much discussion it was decided to adhere to the principle of stupidity. So, to reduce confusion, it is suggested that the bibliographical entries for legal materials follow the same format as footnote entries.

When referencing court cases in the *body of the text* and in *explanatory footnotes* underline the name of the case; for ordinary footnote and bibliographic entries, this is not necessary. Whenever possible cite the official report of the jurisdiction. For United States Supreme Court opinions the official report (U.S.) alone, without accompanying parallel citations, is usually preferred.

U.S. Supreme Court
Footnote: 47. Securities and Exchange Commission v. Chenery Corporation, 318 U.S. 80 (1943).
Bibliography: same as footnote

U.S. Supreme Court (Reporter's Name)
Footnote: 48. Calder v. Bull, 3 U.S. (3 Dall.) 386 (1798).
Bibliography: same as footnote

Federal Cases (F. Cas.)
Footnote: 49. Pritchard v. Georgetown, 19 F. Cas. 1348 (C.C.D.C. 1819) (No. 11,437).
Bibliography: same as footnote

---

3. Melone and Kalvelage, *Primer on Constitutional Law*, pp. 52–54.

Federal Reporter (F.)
Footnote: 50.   National Labor Relations Board v. Rich's Precision Foundry, Inc.,
                667 F.2d 613 (7th Cir. 1981).
Bibliography: same as footnote

Federal Supplement (F. Supp.)
Footnote: 51.   Diamond v. Federal Bureau of Investigation, 532 F. Supp. 216
                (S.D. N.Y. 1981).
Bibliography: same as footnote

Federal Rules Decision (F.R.D.)
Footnote: 52.   Johnson v. North Carolina State Highway Patrol, 91 F.R.D. 406
                (1980).
Bibliography: same as footnote

American Law Reports (A.L.R.)
Footnote: 53.   Annot., 58 A. L.R. Fed. 834 (1980).
Bibliography: same as footnote

State Cases
    Cite both the official and West reports. If a state does not employ an official
reporter system or if the official reports are unavailable, cite the appropriate West
reporter and include the state name.
Footnote: 54.   People v. Savino, 44 N.Y. 2d 669, 376 N.E. 2d 196 (1978).
Bibliography: same as footnote
Footnote: 55.   Agrico Chemical Co. v. Department of Environmental Regulation,
                406 So.2d 478 (Fla. Dist. Ct. App. 1981).
Bibliography: same as footnote

Federal Register (Fed. Reg.)
Footnote: 56.   Smoking Aboard Aircraft, 46 Fed. Reg. 45,934 (1981).
Bibliography: same as footnote

Code of Federal Regulations (C.F.R.)
Footnote: 57.   Smoking Aboard Aircraft, 14 C.F.R. § 252.2(1981).
Bibliography: same as footnote

Legal Encyclopedias
Footnote: 58.   27 AM. JR. 2D *Eminent Domain* §474 (1966).
Bibliography: same as footnote
Footnote: 59.   101A C.J.S. *Zoning and Land Planning* § 21(1979).
Bibliography: same as footnote

Comment: The citation for legal encyclopedias differs significantly from that
                  recommended for nonlegal ones. See, for example, footnote
                  numbers 22 and 23.

Federal Statute

Footnote: 60.   *Administrative Procedure Act*, Publ. L. No. 404, 60 Stat. 237
                  (1946).
Bibliography: same as footnote
Comment: Whenever possible cite the official or one of the unofficial codes
                  rather than the statute.

Federal Code

Footnote: 61.   42 U.S.C. § 7407(b) (Supp. IV 1980).
Bibliography: same as footnote
Footnote: 62.   42 U.S.C.S. § 7407(b) (Law. Co-op. 1982).
Bibliography: same as footnote
Footnote 63.   42 U.S.C.A. § 7407(b) (West 1981 Supp. Pamph.).
Bibliography: same as footnote
Comment: If the statute in question is commonly cited with its official or
                  popular name, it is recommended that it be so cited, for example:
                  Comprehensive Employment and Training Act, § 29 U.S.C.
                  (1978) § 834 (Supp. IV 1980).

State Code

Footnote: 64.   IND. ADMIN. R. tit 16, § 16–10–2–6–B5(Burns 1978).
Bibliography: same as footnote

Federal Administrative Decisions—Official

Footnote: 65.   Baker Protective Services, Inc., 78 F.C.C. 2d 373 (1980).
Bibliography: same as footnote
Footnote: 66.   Lindberg & Sons, Inc., v. Chicago & North Western Transporta-
                  tion Company, et. al., 353 I.C.C. 283 (1977).
Comment: Note that the format for reporting official administrative agency
                  decisions is identical to court decisions.

Federal Administrative Decisions—Looseleaf Publications

Footnote: 67.   *NRDC* v. *EPA*, Nos. 80–1313, et. al., ENV'T REP. (BNA) Vol.
                  12, no. 2, at 61 (May 8, 1981).
Bibliography: same as footnote
Comment: The editors of *A Uniform System of Citation*, 13th edition, recom-
                  mend that looseleaf service citations contain: volume, abbreviated
                  title, publisher name, subdivision, and date. Researchers may want

to consult rule 18.2 of *A Uniform System of Citation*, 13th edition, for a guide to abbreviations.

Law Journal Article
Footnote: 68. Braeman, *Overview of FOIA Administration in Government*, 34 AD. L. REV. 119 (1982).
Bibliography: same as footnote
Comment: Compare the form of legal journal footnotes to that recommended for nonlegal journals: see footnote 18.

U.S. Constitution
Footnote: 69. U.S. Const. art. I, § 9.
Bibliography: Need no reference in bibliography.

SECOND OR LATER REFERENCES TO FOOTNOTES

It is possible to refer several times to the same footnote. The general rules are:

1. For references to the same work with no intervening footnotes simply use the Latin term "Ibid.," meaning "in the same place."
2. For second references with no intervening footnote, but with a different page of the same work, state Ibid. and the page number. Example: Ibid., p. 87.
3. For second references with intervening footnotes, state: author's last name, but not first name or initials unless another author of the same name is cited; a shortened title of the work; and the specific page number.

Following are examples of second citations of a representative number of works.

Book
First Citation: 1. Guy Benveniste, *Regulation and Planning: The Case of Environmental Politics* (San Francisco, Calif.: Boyd & Fraser Publishing Company, 1981), p. 122.
Second Citation: 7. Benveniste, *Regulation and Planning*, p. 131.

Journal Article
First Citation: 2. David H. Rosenbloom, "The Judicial Response to the Rise of the American Administrative State," *American Review of Public Administration* 15 (Spring 1981): 40.
Second Citation: 8. Rosenbloom, "Judicial Response," p. 48.

Federal Documents
First Citation: 3. U.S. Congress, Senate, Senator Proxmire Explanation for Voting Against Budget Resolution, 97th Cong., 2nd sess., 22 June 1982, *Congressional Record* 128: S 7279.
Second Citation: 5. U.S. Congress, Senate, Proxmire Explanation, S 7280.

Court Case

First Citation: 4. Far East Conference v. United States, 342 U.S. 570(1952).

Second Citation: 6. 342 U.S. at 571. *Or* 342 U.S. 570,571.

SCIENTIFIC REFERENCE FORM

Some scholarly journals have adopted the scientific reference format. Instead of the conventionally numbered footnote, scientific notations employ parenthetic references that include the author's last name, the year of publication, and the pagination; e.g., "Possessing experience in complex interactions, lawyers and businessmen are more likely than others to have an appreciation for bargaining, compromise, and generally the art of the possible (Eulau and Sprague, 1964:144)." Today all the political science journals published by Sage Publications employ this method, and *The American Political Science Review* and *The Western Political Quarterly* have switched from the conventional format described earlier to the scientific reference style demonstrated in the rest of this chapter.

Increasingly instructors are either permitting or encouraging the adoption of the scientific style for student papers. As can be observed from the few examples to be presented, the scientific format is simpler to use than the conventional format. Its principal disadvantage is the interruption to the flow of ideas and sentences caused by the intrusion in the body of the text of author names, publication dates, and pagination. The exact format for scientific reference varies somewhat from journal to journal and from one science discipline to another. The format recommended here is a hybrid variety devised for simplicity.

Guide to Scientific References

1. All but explanatory footnotes (discursive comments) are placed in the body of the text.
2. Parenthetical references include author, year of publication, and pagination.
3. Repeat earlier citation for second or later references.
4. All sources cited in the text are listed at the end of the paper under "References."
5. Explanatory or discursive comments are referenced in the conventional style with footnote numbers placed in the body of the text and the comments placed together at the end of the manuscript immediately before the References. These are titled "Notes."

Author's Name Not in Body of Text

Comment: Author's last name is followed by a comma, the year of publication, colon, and page number if referencing particular page(s).

Example: . . . conventional wisdom supports the proposition that lawyers exercise considerable influence as the high priests of American politics (Matthews, 1954:30).

More Than One Author
Comment: Simply join the two names with the conjunctive "and." If more than two authors employ "et. al."
Example: (Schmidhauser and Berg, 1972:191).
Example: (Brady et al., 1973:870).

Multiple References
Comment: Often researchers point to several texts supporting the same or a similar statement. In such instances references are joined by semicolons.
Example: However, in recent years several roll call studies indicate that lawyer-legislators do not vote as a cohesive bloc (Derge, 1959; Schmidhauser and Berg, 1972; Brady et al., 1973).

Author's Name in the Body of Text
Comment: When the author's name is in the body of the text follow the name with the year and pagination.
Example: Schiengold (1974:13–22) points out that law as an ideology creates . . .

References to Same Author and Same Year
Comment: At times scholars will publish several articles or books in the same year and the researcher may want to cite some or all of them without confusion. This problem is eliminated by inserting "a," "b," "c," etc. in both the *manuscript* and *references* at the end of the paper.
Example: (Schmidhauser, 1973a: 183).
(Schmidhauser, 1973b: 17).
(Schmidhauser 1973c: 401).

Court Cases Cited in Body of Text
Comment: As with other references, court cases including administrative agency decisions should be included in the body of the text. The case name is underlined (italized) followed by the date in parentheses. For second and later references repeat the case name but delete the date.
Example: . . . the decision in *Goldberg* v. *Kelly* (1970) holds that welfare recipients are entitled to due process of law.

REFERENCES at the End of the Paper
All cited materials are listed together at the end of the paper in alphabetical order by author. In a Bibliography all relevant sources consulted in researching and writing the paper are included. However, in a Reference only those materials actually cited in the text of the paper are included. Also, include the names of all authors in multiple authored works. This rule applies to books or articles with three or more authors as well as works with fewer authors. The reference form for articles, books, associations as author, and dissertations or theses differ. Note each in the sample references presented below.

Judicial opinions, including administrative law opinions, should be listed in alphabetical order with full citation to volume, reporter series, page, and date. This list should appear immediately following the REFERENCES at the end of the paper under the separate title, CASES CITED.

Books:

Durkheim, Emile (1958). *Professional Ethics and Civil Morals.* Glencoe, Ill.: Free Press.

Eulau, Heinz and John D. Sprague (1964). *Lawyers in Politics: A Study of Professional Convergence.* Indianapolis: Bobbs-Merrill.

McLaughlin, Andrew Cummingham (1972a). *The Courts, the Constitution, and Parties: Studies in Constitutional History and Politics.* New York: Da Capo Press.

———— (1972b). *The Foundations of American Constitutionalism.* Gloucester, Mass.: P. Smith.

Articles:

Dyer, James A., (1976). "Do Lawyers Vote Differently? A Study of Voting on No-Fault Insurance." *Journal of Politics* 38 (May): 452–456.

Green Justin J., John R. Schmidhauser, Larry L. Berg, and David Brady (1973). "Lawyers in Congress: A New Look at Some Old Assumptions." *Western Political Quarterly* 26 (September): 440–452.

Association:

American Bar Association (1975). *Report of American Bar Associaiton.* Chicago: American Bar Foundation.

Theses or Dissertations:

Wells, Richard Sutton (1963). "The Legal Profession and Political Ideology: The Case of the Carr Law Firm of Manchester, Iowa." Ph.D. dissertation. Iowa City: University of Iowa.

Court Cases:

Goldberg v. *Kelly,* 397 U.S. 254, 1970.
United States v. *Du Pont,* 353 U.S. 586, 1957.

6

Glossary

ABROGATE. The repeal, annulment, or destruction of an order or rule of a lower power by the same or higher authority.

ACCUSATORIAL SYSTEM. The legal system which presumes that a person is innocent until proven guilty. The outstanding feature of Anglo-American criminal justice placing the burden of proof upon the accuser.

AD HOC. For a special or one time purpose; temporary and not permanent.

ADJECTIVE LAW. Generic term referring to rules under which courts or agencies conduct their affairs; procedural as opposed to substantive law.

ADMINISTRATIVE LAW. The growing branch of public law dealing with the rules and regulations promulgated by government agencies.

ADMINISTRATIVE LAW JUDGE. The official title for federal hearing officers since 1972. Cf. Hearing officer.

ADMINISTRATIVE PROCEDURE ACT (APA). The 1946 act of Congress (as amended) which provides (with exceptions) for processes to be followed by administrative agencies and departments in rule making adjudication, the handling of public information, use of hearing examiners, some procedural protections, separation of prosecuting and adjudicating functions and hearings, and related matters. Many states have comparable acts.

ADMIRALTY LAW. The branch of the law concerned with maritime matters.

AD VALOREM. Latin meaning according to value. An ad valorem tax is a levy on the value of something rather than a fixed tax regardless of value. For example, if an ad valorem tax on a diamond ring worth $100 were $5, the tax on a $10,000 ring would then be $500. The tax varies according to the worth or value of the item rather than a fixed tax of, say, $75 for all diamond rings.

ADVISORY OPINION. A judicial ruling in the absence of an actual case or controversy; a ruling in a hypothetical case without bona fide litigants.

AGENCY. (A) May refer to an administrative body of government. (B) A relationship in which one party acts on behalf of another; the former is authorized by the latter.

AGENCY ACTION COMMITTED TO AGENCY DISCRETION BY LAW. Actions which the legislature indicates should be exclusively decided by an administrative agency and are not reviewed by the courts unless there is a compelling reason to do so such as a constitutional question.

AGENCY ADVICE. If agency guidance is sought in a matter, there may be questions as to whether that advice is reliable. Although it is generally considered reliable, courts have suggested that this is not necessarily the case in law. Cf. Estoppel.

AMICUS CURIAE. Latin for ''friend of the court.'' Normally an outside interest not directly a party to the suit usually presents a brief that provides information and argument relevant to a court in its deliberation on matters of law.

ANALYTICAL JURISPRUDENCE. A school of jurisprudence that attempts to systematize the law logically. Outstanding proponents include Hans Kelsen, John Austin, and H.L.A. Hart.

ANSWER. Usually a written statement or pleading by the defendant responding to the plaintiff's charges.

APA. See Administrative Procedure Act.

APPEAL. A generic term referring to the movement of court proceedings from an inferior to a superior court. Depending on the context, the term may refer to a technical method of moving a case to a superior court.

APPELLANT. The party who takes a case from a lower court to a superior court to seek review of the lower court decision.

APPELLATE COURT. A court possessing the authority to review and sustain or reverse the decisions of lower courts.

APPELLEE. The party in a suit against whom the appeal to a superior court is taken; the party with an interest in sustaining the lower court judgment.

ARBITRATION. A third party hearing/settlement of a dispute between contending parties. The decision of the arbitrator(s) may be binding upon the participants.

ARGUENDO. During the course of argument to make the assumption that a statement is true, although it may be true or false. A method of illustrating a line of reasoning found in many judicial opinions.

ASSUMPSIT. An action for recovery of damages based on nonfulfillment of a promise, parole, or contract (but not of record or under seal).

AUDI ALTERAM PARTEM. The principle or rule that in a legal matter both sides of the question must be heard. The parties are to be given adequate notice and opportunity to be heard.

BANKRUPTCY. A legal procedure under federal law by which a person is relieved of all debts after placing all property under the court's authority. An organization may be reorganized or terminated by the court in order to pay off creditors.

BAR. The community of attorneys permitted to practice law in a particular jurisdiction or court.

BEST EVIDENCE. A rule by which the "best evidence available" should be presented in a legal proceeding rather than lesser evidence, and also in lieu of the original evidence, if the latter is unavailable. The "best evidence" rule requires, for instance, that when referring to a written document, the document itself be produced in court. It is not sufficient to simply "talk" about the document; one must present the writing in court, if available. Nevertheless, if that document cannot be found, other evidence of its existence can be substituted.

BIAS. Interest or prejudice. Central to doctrine regarding bias is the concept that a judge should not have a financial stake in the outcome of a decision or a personal antipathy for a litigant. However, the legal requirement prohibiting bias does not preclude the judge's having a predetermined substantive view of a matter.

BLUE LAW. Legislative enactment forbidding all or certain business activity on Sundays.

BONA FIDE. Latin for "good faith." A term referring to acting in good faith; without trickery, deceit, fraud, or dishonesty.

BREACH OF CONTRACT. The nonperformance of the terms of a legally binding oral or written agreement.

BRIEF. (A) The oral or written argument presented by counsel to a court. (B) A summary of the pertinent elements of a court opinion written by a student as a study guide and aid.

BURDEN OF PROOF. The matter of who has the primary responsibility to prove or substantiate an allegation. Mainly it entails (1) producing evidence of a particular alleged fact, and (2) establishing its truth. In administrative law this burden usually rests with the agency.

CALENDAR. A list of cases in the order in which they are to be heard during a court term. Sometimes known as a court docket or trial list.

CANON LAW. The well developed body of laws governing ecclesiastical matters of a Christian church; usually thought of in relationship to the Roman Catholic Church.

CASE AND CONTROVERSY. Legal dispute with bona fide adversaries involving live and real issues. Not hypothetical or abstract issues, rights, or claims to be protected.

CASEBOOK. A law textbook containing leading edited judicial opinions on a particular legal subject. Cases are usually arranged chronologically by subject. First casebook published in 1871 authored by a dean of the Harvard Law School: Langdell, *Selection of Cases on the Law of Contracts.*

CASE LAW. The law as handed down in written judicial opinions.

CASE METHOD. A rigorous and dominant approach to legal education stressing the reading and in-depth analysis of leading judicial opinions. The growth of the law is traced through the reading of the cases. Professors employ the Socratic questioning method in connection with the cases. Critics of the case method contend that it produces socially myopic attorneys.

CAUSE OF ACTION. The existence of sufficient facts to warrant a law suit brought by a plaintiff.

CEASE AND DESIST ORDER. An administrative order by an agency that requires an individual, firm, or union to cease violation of a rule or law. It is an important agency enforcement tool and violations may result in a penalty.

CERTIFICATION. A method of appeal by which a lower court requests a higher court to answer certain questions of law so that the lower court may make a correct decision in light of the answer provided.

CERTIORARI, WRIT OF. An order from a superior to an inferior court to send the entire record of a case to the superior court for review. A discretionary writ employed by the U.S. Supreme Court. In Britain it is an important remedy for bringing agencies to heel for abuse of power. In the United States it is not usually applicable to agencies.

CHANCERY, COURT OF. An old English court dealing with equity matters. In America most state governments have merged the chancery and law courts into one.

CHARTER. A document emanating from a government's granting certain rights, liberties, or powers to an organization, colony, local government, corporation, or people; e.g., city charter, colonial charter, corporation charter, Magna Carta.

CHIEF JUSTICE. The person appointed by the President with the advice and consent of the Senate to head the U.S. Supreme Court.

CIVIL ACTION. A lawsuit typically brought by a private party for the redress of a noncriminal act. Usually the plaintiff seeks money damages for the wrongful conduct of the defendant. For example, suits in negligence, contract, or defamation.

CIVIL LAW. (A) The system of jurisprudence based upon Roman law found in most Western European nation-states. It is distinct from the common law. (B) In common law countries civil law refers to noncriminal legal matters.

CLASS ACTION SUIT. A legal suit brought by one person on behalf of himself/herself and all others similarly situated. For example, John Doe, as representative of the class of all persons similarly situated, and for himself, Plaintiff, v. Paul Smith, in his capacity as Chief of Police of the City of XYZ, Defendant.

CLEAR AND CONVINCING EVIDENCE. See Substantial evidence.

CLEARLY ERRONEOUS RULE. An appellate court should not reverse the lower court or agency as to findings except where the latter's findings have been patently incorrect, i.e. clearly erroneous.

COMMON LAW. The system of law created by the English courts and brought to America by the colonists. Judges are said to find the law in the customs and habits of the people. It is largely judge–made law as distinct from statutory law made by legislators. Its chief competitor is the Roman-founded civil law system of Western Europe.

COMPETENT EVIDENCE. Evidence that is admissible in a jury trial under the rules of evidence. This is not generally required in agency litigation except that under the residuum rule there should be some evidence of this character. Cf. Legal residuum rule.

COMPLAINT. The plaintiff's initial pleading that frames the issues in the suit.

CONCURRENT JURISDICTION. The authority possessed by two or more courts to hear cases on a given subject.

CONCURRENT POWER. The political authority to exercise independent power by more than one government on the same subject matter. For example, the taxing powers in a federal system.

CONFLICT OF LAWS. Refers to the field of law dealing with the situation in which a judge must choose among the laws of more than one jurisdiction as to which should apply in a particular case.

CONSPIRACY. Two or more persons acting together to accomplish a criminal objective or to pursue a noncriminal purpose in an unlawful or criminal manner.

CONSTITUTIONAL COURTS. A court named in a constitution or a court given certain protections independent of the other political branches of government. For the U.S. government, a constitutional court is one authorized under Article III of the Constitution or designated by the Congress as an Article III court. Article III courts are protected as to jurisdiction, appointment, and tenure.

CONSTITUTIONALISM. The principle of the rule of law under which the rulers abide by certain rules limiting their official conduct in return for the right to exercise authority.

CONTEMPT. An act that in some way obstructs or denigrates the dignity of a court, a legislative body, or an administrative agency. Usually a punishable offense.

CONTENTIEUX DE L'ANNULATION. In French administrative law, litigation in which the plaintiff seeks annulment of an administrative act on the grounds of its illegality.

CONTENTIEUX DE LA REPRESSION. In French administrative law the only area in which criminal jurisdiction is conveyed to the administrative courts and where action is brought by government against the individual. It applies only restrictively in cases of damage done to some categories of public property, primarily waterways.

CONTENTIEUX DE PLEINE JURIDICTION. In French administrative law, litigation in which the plaintiff seeks not only annulment of an administrative act but damages as well.

COOPERATIVE FEDERALISM. A general approach to the American federal system that views the relationship between the national and state governments as a working partnership by which the mutual interests of both may be satisfied. Some take a more extreme view by stressing the ''necessity'' of national supremacy.

CORPUS JURIS CIVILIS. The body of Roman law including the Digest, the Institutes, the Code, and the Novels of Justinian. Latin for the body of civil law.

COUNT. Separate and independent claims or charges in a civil or criminal matter. A criminal indictment, for example, may contain many counts which if the prosecution should lose on one or more, it will still have others on which to convict.

COUNTERCLAIM. Constituting a separate cause of action, it is a claim made by the defendant against the plaintiff. Such a practice occurs in civil suits.

COURT OF LAST RESORT. A popular term referring to a court from which there is no appeal.

CREATION OF STANDARDS. Sometime requirement that the legislature set standards when delegating powers to agencies. Although legislative bodies should establish standards or limits attending delegation, this requirement is rather in limbo. Increasingly courts require agencies themselves to establish standards as a requirement of due process.

CRIME. A violation of government's penal laws. The offense is against society and not just a violation of another's individual rights.

CULPABLE. A term referring to blame-worthy or wrongful conduct. Faultable.

CUMULATIVE EVIDENCE. Evidence which merely corroborates what is already sufficiently proven.

CURIA. Latin for court.

DAMAGES. Money awarded by a court to a plaintiff for the wrongful conduct of the defendant.

DECLARATORY JUDGMENT. A judicial determination of the legal rights of the parties involved in an actual case or controversy, but where the court does not require the parties to abide by the judgment. Differs from an advisory opinion because there is an actual case or controversy.

DECLARATORY ORDER. Administrative agency judgment comparable to a declaratory judgment by a court. Authorized by the Administrative Procedure Act, it helps remedy uncertainties of agency advice and estoppel. Nevertheless, agencies have often declined to issue them on the grounds of discretion to do so in the APA.

DECREE. A court order or sentence specifying the details of a legal settlement, e.g., terms of alimony or child custody. A consent decree is an agreement among the parties to conduct their affairs in a certain way. It cannot be amended without the consent of both parties.

DE FACTO. Refers to the existence of something in fact or in reality as distinguished from de jure, by right. For example, segregation in housing due to custom but not the result of official government action is often termed de facto segregation.

DEFENDANT. In a court case, the one against whom a civil or criminal charge is brought.

DE JURE. Refers to lawful, rightful, or legitimate; contrast with de facto. For example, segregation in public education mandated by state law was known as de jure segregation.

DELEGATION. In administrative law the grant by a legislature to an agency of authority to legislate or otherwise act including in theory an indication of limits.

DELIBERATION. The process of weighing reasons or evidence for or against a course of action. Usually applies to the work of a jury when determining guilt or innocence.

DE MINIMUS NON CURAT LEX. Latin term meaning that the law is not concerned with trivialities.

DEMURRER. A legal procedure permitting counsel to object to the sufficiency of a legal cause of action contained in the pleadings of the other side. Even if the act complained of did in fact occur, the law as presented by the other side does not cover that situation.

DE NOVO. A Latin term for anew, once more, again. Often applies to a case being retried upon order of an appellate court. Some court systems permit de novo appeals.

DEPOSITION. A legal process to record the testimony of a witness outside of the courtroom. Usually both plaintiff and defendant attorneys are present and participate.

DEVELOPMENT OF THE RECORD. With a view to court review or appeal, regulatory agency decisions and rule-making should be accompanied by a meticulous record of the process. See Record.

DICTA. See Obiter dicta.

DISCOVERY. The mutual disclosure by the parties of pertinent facts, documents, and other data as part of the pretrial procedure.

DIVERSITY JURISDICTION. Refers to the authority of federal courts to hear cases involving citizens of different states.

DOCKET. A listing of cases to be heard by a court.

DUAL FEDERALISM. The general approach to the American federal system that views the relationship between the national and state governments as adversarial. Best represented by the states' rights position that views the powers of the central government as strictly limited by the enumerated provisions in the Constitution; all other powers are reserved to the states by way of the Tenth Amendment.

EMINENT DOMAIN. The right and ability of government to take private property for public use.

EN BANC. Sometimes appearing as *En Banke*, meaning all the judges of a court or all jury members sitting together to hear a case.

EQUITY. The administration of justice based upon principles of fairness rather than strictly applied rules found in the common law. Because the common law courts of England became too rigid, equity courts were created; in the U.S., courts of law and courts of equity have largely been merged.

ERROR, WRIT OF. A method of appeal by which an appellate court orders a lower court to send a case to the higher court for review of alleged mistakes made by the lower court. Matters of law, not of fact, are reviewed. The U.S. Supreme Court no longer employs this appeal method.

ESCHEAT. If the rightful owner or heir of property cannot be located, the property goes to the state.

ESTOPPEL. Equitable doctrine whereby a private party who gives advice or direction cannot act against the person relying on such information on the ground that the person's agent lacked authority. Government, however, frequently is not subject to estoppel. In Schwartz's words, this application ''has all the beauty of logic and all the ugliness of injustice.''

EVIDENCE. Any sort of proof which is legally presented in a case.

EXCEPTIS EXCIPIENDIS. Latin for the due exceptions being made.

EXCLUSIONARY RULES. Those rules which exclude from jury consideration certain kinds of evidence, the most important of which are said to be hearsay or that which is illegally obtained.

EXCLUSIVE JURISDICTION. The sole authority vested in one court to hear a case on a given subject matter; e.g., for the U.S. Supreme Court, suits between and among the states, foreign ambassadors, bankruptcy, and prosecutions of federal criminal law.

EXCLUSIVENESS OF THE RECORD. The principle that agency and court decisions must be drawn only from material presented in court and subject to rebuttal and which are a part of the written proceedings.

EXCLUSIVE POWER. The sole exercise of authority by one governmental body; e.g., the U.S. national government possesses sole authority to make war.

EXECUTIVE AGREEMENT. An international agreement made by the President under the constitutional authority as commander-in-chief and in the capacity as the nation's spokesperson in foreign affairs. These agreements do not require senatorial approval as is the case for a treaty but are usually pursuant to an act of Congress.

EXECUTIVE ORDERS. A directive from the President requiring the implementation of policy. The source of this authority stems from congressional authorization with the President as chief executive spelling out the details of policy implementation.

EXECUTIVE PRIVILEGE. The not infrequent refusal of the executive branch to disclose information to Congress or to others. The U.S. Supreme Court acknowledged but limited this in *U.S. v. Nixon*, 114 U.S. 683 (1974).

EXHAUSTION. In administrative law this term means that all the administrative steps or procedures or appeals have been taken to resolve a matter. See also Ripeness; Standing to sue.

EX PARTE. A judicial hearing when only one party is present, such as when the appellant is in prison.

EX POST FACTO LAW. Latin for a law "after the fact." An ex post facto law attempts to make an act a crime that was not a crime when it was done. Specifically prohibited by the U.S. Constitution.

EX. REL. An abbreviation for *Ex Relatione* meaning upon relation or information. A designation appearing in case titles indicating that the suit is instituted by a state but at the instigation or insistence of an individual; e.g., *Missouri ex. rel. Gaines* v. *S.W. Canada*. The state of Missouri is bringing the suit at the instigation of Lloyd Gaines against S.W. Canada.

EXTRADITION. The surrender of a fugitive by one jurisdiction to another.

FEDERATION. A structure of government dividing powers between the central and state governments; both the state and national governments operate directly upon the people.

FIDUCIARY. A relationship in which one person acts in a position of trust for another. Sometimes involves management of money or property.

FINDING. A court's decision on an issue of fact.

FINDINGS OF FACT. The primary physical events pertinent to a legal issue. Distinction is made between first order and second order facts. The former is primary, while the latter may entail a secondary interpretation. Appellate courts will usually decline to review first order factual findings, will sometimes review second order findings, and will much more readily review findings of law.

FINDINGS OF LAW. The legal interpretation of a court or agency in regard to some matter. A reviewing court will be more likely to entertain review of findings of law than of findings of fact.

FISHING EXPEDITION. A wide search for evidence of crime through subpoenas by an administrative agency. Denied by Justice Holmes in *FTC* v.

American Tobacco Co. (1924), but sanctioned after a decision by Justice Rutledge in *Okla. Press Publishing Co.* v. *Walling* (1946).

FREEDOM OF INFORMATION ACT. Federal law of 1976 which provided that a great measure of agency action should be available to the public. It is an amendment to the Administrative Procedure Act.

HABEAS CORPUS, WRIT OF. A writ directing that a person held in custody be brought before the court to determine if he or she is being lawfully held.

HEARING. A proceeding in an administrative agency which is substantially like a trial. It centers upon issues of fact.

HEARING EXAMINER. See Hearing Officer.

HEARING OFFICER. Agency officers who hear "cases" and render decisions. Under the Administrative Procedure Act they are to be sufficiently independent in order to function fairly. In the national government and many state governments they are now called administrative law judges.

HEARSAY EVIDENCE. Secondhand information. When a witness relates something which others have told him rather than something he personally knows, that evidence is called hearsay.

HEARSAY RULE. A rule which, with some exceptions, prohibits testimony on matters about which the witness does not have first hand knowledge, sometimes called secondhand evidence.

IN CAMERA. Latin for "in chambers." A device by which judges hear a case or part of a case in their chambers without spectators.

INDEPENDENT AGENCY. A government agency which is not under an executive department. Regulatory agencies are included but the term usually decribes agencies which perform a service. An example is the General Services Administration.

INDEPENDENT REGULATORY COMMISSIONS. Government agencies, not under executive departments, which regulate aspects of the economy. They are usually headed by commissions of five or seven members. Examples include the Federal Trade Commission, the Federal Reserve Board, and the Federal Energy Regulatory Commission.

INFORMAL RULE-MAKING. See Notice and comment rule-making.

IN FORMA PAUPERIS. Latin for "in the manner of a pauper." It is a device for indigents to sue without liability for costs. Provided for by U.S. statutory law permitting any citizen upon the execution of an oath to enter proceedings in any federal court. The most celebrated case reaching the U.S. Supreme Court in this manner is *Gideon* v. *Wainwright*. (1963).

INJUNCTION. A court order directing someone to do something or refrain from doing something.

IN PERSONAM. Latin for "toward a person" or individual. It is a legal action taken against an individual and not against the whole world.

IN RE. Latin referring "to the matter of." Employed in entitling judicial proceedings where there are no adversary parties; e.g., *In re: Jones*.

IN REM. A legal action to enforce property rights against the whole world and not one brought to enforce a legal right against individuals (In personam).

INTERLOCUTORY. Temporary, not final, provisional.

INTERLOCUTORY ORDER. An order made in the course of a trial which settles an "intervening matter" but not the main substance of the case itself.

INTERSTATE COMPACT. An agreement between two or more states, ratified by law of each state and approved by Congress.

INTESTATE. Dying without a will.

IPSE DIXIT. Latin for "he himself said it." Depends on the authority of the one who said it.

IPSO FACTO. Latin for "by the fact itself." The fact speaks for itself.

JUDICIAL NOTICE. Court acknowledgement of commonly known or undisputed facts in a matter without their being presented as evidence, e.g., highway I–70 runs generally east and west.

JUDICIAL REVIEW. (A) The power of a court to examine legislative enactments and acts of executive officials to determine their validity with respect to a written constitution; e.g., *Marbury* v. *Madison* (1803); (B) Court review of agency decisions and actions.

JUDICIAL SELF-RESTRAINT. The position that judges should refrain from substituting their values for those of political decisionmakers who are closer to the sentiments of the people. Operationally, the U.S. Supreme Court has devised various techniques of restraint so as to defer to other decisionmakers.

JURISPRUDENCE. (A) The philosophy or science of law. (B) Sometimes refers to a body of law. (C) In civil law countries it refers to cases and decisions.

JUS SANGUINIS. Latin for "law of blood." Refers to gaining citizenship by virtue of being born of parents who are citizens.

JUS SOLI. Latin for the "law of land." Refers to gaining citizenship by virtue of place or country in which a person is born.

LARCENY. The theft of the personal property of another. The act of stealing.

LEGAL RESIDUUM RULE. A rule that an agency decision should not be upheld by a reviewing court if there is no "competent evidence" in the record to support it. There must be at least a "residuum of legal evidence" in support of the decision along with whatever other evidence has been admitted. It is followed usually but not always in federal cases and in most states.

LEGISLATIVE COURTS. Courts established by the legislature. For the U.S. government, legislative courts are not protected by Article III. See Constitutional Courts.

LEGISLATIVE INTENT. Refers to the motives of legislators when enacting a law. Usually involves a reading and interpreting by a court of the legislative history of a statute.

LIABILITY. Responsibility for performing a legally enforceable duty or obligation resulting from the commission of a wrongful act.

LIEN. The legal right to hold property of another as security against a debt. If the debt is not paid or discharged, the property may be sold to satisfy the obligation.

LIS INTER PARTES. Latin for "suit between the parties."

LITIGANT. An active participant in a lawsuit; e.g., *Smith* v. *Jones*. Both Smith and Jones are litigants.

LOCUS STANDI. The status by which one has the right to appear at a court or an agency. Cf. Standing to sue.

MALPRACTICE. Refers to professional misconduct or the below-standard performance of professional skills. Usually applies to suits against physicians and lawyers.

MALUM IN SE. Latin for ''inherently wrong.''

MALUM PROHIBITUM. Latin for ''wrong because it is prohibited.''

MANDAMUS, WRIT OF. Latin for ''we command.'' It is a court order ordering a public official or government agency to perform a certain act. It may apply to all branches of government.

MARTIAL LAW. The displacement of civilian law and government by the military. Rules usually depend solely upon the commands of the military ruler in charge and often tend to be arbitrary. Often imposed in time of war, insurrection, or coup d'etat.

MAXIM. A certain precept or axiom of law applied to all cases covered by its usage.

MEMORANDUM DECISION. A court ruling giving only what has been decided and what should be done but without the reasons for the decision.

MINISTERIAL. The carrying out of orders without making policy choices. No exercise of judgment or discretion.

MISDEMEANOR. A criminal offense designated by statute to be of a lesser nature than a felony. Penalties are relatively minor.

MODEL STATE ADMINISTRATIVE PROCEDURE ACT. A draft law first recommended in 1946 by the Commission on Uniform State Laws. It was revised in 1961 and again in 1981 and, in one version or another, has been enacted in 21 states.

MOOT. A discussion or argument of a hypothetical situation.

MOOT QUESTION. In a lawsuit, when the situation changes so that the relief sought is no longer applicable. For example, if during the course of a lengthy lawsuit for admission to a professional school, the student petitioner, who has been admitted pending decision, in fact completes school, the question of admission becomes moot.

MOTION. A request by an attorney to the judge to take some action; e.g., dismiss the case.

NATURAL JUSTICE. In British practice the idea that there are two essential requirements: (1) that the judge be disinterested and unbiased and (2) that parties have adequate notice and a chance to be heard.

NATURAL LAW. A higher law transcending positive law; coming from God, nature, the universe, or reason; it lacks the ability to enforce commands.

NEGLIGENCE. A subfield of tort law dealing with cases in which it is alleged that the defendant failed to exercise reasonable care, thereby resulting in injury or harm to another or to some object.

NEMOJUDEX IN CAUSA. A Latin term specifying the maxim that a judge should not act in a matter in which the judge has an interest; or that the judge must be disinterested and unbiased. British writers call it the first and most fundamental principle of natural justice. (Sometimes cited as *Nemo judex in re sua* or in other variant forms.)

NISI PRIUS. Latin meaning if not, unless before. Usually employed when referring to jury trial before a single judge as distinguished from an appellate court.

NOLO CONTENDERE. Latin for "no contest." Without directly admitting guilt, it is a plea in a criminal proceeding in which the defendant does not offer a defense. A sentence is then handed down with the assumption of guilt.

NOTICE. Communication by an authorized body to a person about a law suit in which the person is a principal or has an interest.

NOTICE AND COMMENT RULE-MAKING. The process of making rules as described in section 553 of the Administrative Procedure Act. It involves notice of a pending rule, opportunity for comment, making the rule, and opportunity for registering dissent.

NOVUS HOMO. Latin for "new man." Applied in reference to a person pardoned of a crime.

OBITER DICTA. Those parts of the reasoning of a judicial opinion which are not directly pertinent to the result reached by the court. It is extra and unnecessary verbiage included for a variety of reasons.

OFFICIAL NOTICE. Taking cognizance of obvious facts by an agency. Comparable to judicial notice for a court. The Administrative Procedure Act specifies that an interested party has a right to show that what has been noticed is in fact otherwise. Cf. Judicial notice.

OMBUDSMAN. An officer authorized to hear complaints and to investigate, probe, and publicize, usually without enforcement power.

OPEN MEETING ACTS. See Sunshine laws.

OPINION EVIDENCE. Testimony that the witness is of the opinion that a pertinent fact exists or does not exist.

ORDERS. When an agency establishes a norm via its judicial function, it is known as an order. Cf. Rules.

ORDINANCE. Usually refers to a local law.

PER CURIAM OPINION. A judicial opinion by the whole court expressing the views of the justices collectively.

PETITIONER. The party to a lawsuit who brings the case to a court by way of a petition; e.g., the petition for a writ of certiorari. The party the petition is brought against is called the respondent.

PLAIN MEANING RULE. When the language of a statute is clear and may be interpreted in only one way, a court employing this rule considers only the language and not other sources for assigning meaning.

PLAINTIFF. The party to a conflict who brings a lawsuit against another (defendant).

PLEA. The first pleading made by a defendant; a formal response to a criminal charge, for example, guilty, not guilty, or nolo contendre.

PLEADINGS. The formal and technical written statements made by the litigants framing the issues brought before a court.

POSITIVE LAW. Man-made law enacted by a ruler, judge, or a legislature of some kind.

PRECEDENT. A previously decided judicial opinion which serves as a guide for the decision in a present case. The facts of the past and present cases must be deemed sufficiently similar to serve as a precedent.

PREPONDERANCE OF EVIDENCE. The level of proof sufficient to decide a civil case. In a comparison of evidence, preponderance suggests that which is the more convincing. Cf. Proof beyond a reasonable doubt; Substantial evidence.

PREROGATIVE WRIT. Issued by the courts not as a matter of right, but at court discretion. These are the writs of procedendo, mandamus, prohibition, quo warranto, habeas corpus, and certiorari.

PRIMA FACIE. Latin for "at first sight," on first view. Prima facie evidence is such evidence that, if not later contradicted or in some way explained, is sufficient to sustain one's claim. A prima facie case is one that has proceeded to the point where it will support the charge if not later contradicted.

PRIMARY JURISDICTION. That agency or court which has the right to hear a case initially is said to have primary jurisdiction.

PRIMARY JURISDICTION DOCTRINE. In administrative law a pertinent case is usually dealt with first by the agency (rather than a regular court) unless an overriding reason is present for action by the regular courts. Cf. Exhaustion.

PRIVACY ACTS. Legislation which protects the individual against indiscriminate dissemination of information about him which is held by government or an agency of government.

PRIVATE LAW. (A) Statute dealing with one person or a group. For example, a law passed to compensate Mr. Smith for damage to his property because of Army exercises. (B) A generic term referring to the law governing conflicts among private parties; e.g., contracts, property, torts, divorce.

PROCEDURAL LAW. The various and often complex rules governing the conduct of court cases.

PROCURATURA. In the USSR and the communist world, the office of the prosecutor. It includes the power to pressure for the correct legal conduct of government agencies and may investigate citizens' complaints. Cf. Ombudsman.

PROHIBITION, WRIT OF. A prerogative writ by which a court prohibits a lower court from acting in a matter where it lacks jurisdiction.

PROOF BEYOND A REASONABLE DOUBT. That level of proof or evidence sufficient for a jury to convict in a criminal case. It means that the evidence is sufficient to dispel any "reasonable doubt" as to innocence or guilt. The California penal code describes it thus: ". . . It is that state of the case, which, after the entire comparison and consideration of all the evidence, leaves the minds of jurors in condition that they cannot say they feel an abiding conviction, to a moral certainty, of the truth of the charge." Cf. Preponderance of evidence; Substantial evidence.

PROPERTY. Ownership divided into two major parts. Real property, ownership in land, and personal property, ownership in movable objects or chattels.

PUBLIC INTERVENTION. In agency litigation persons with a sufficient interest in a matter are usually permitted to appear and testify. It is akin to Standing to sue.

PUBLIC LAW. (A) Statute dealing with the society as a whole; e.g., minimum wage laws, energy legislation, reorganization of governmental agencies. In Congress such laws are given a number, e.g., ''Public Law No. 35.'' (B) A generic term referring to laws governing operations of government and the government's relationships with persons; e.g., constitutional law, criminal law, administrative law.

PUNITIVE DAMAGES. Sometimes called ''exemplary damages.'' They are awarded in a civil case for malicious or willful harm inflicted by the defendant. Money damages awarded by a court over and beyond actual and compensatory damages for the harm suffered, and intended to act as a warning and deterrent against future wrongful conduct.

QUAERE. A question or query involving a matter in doubt.

QUASI-JUDICIAL. Actions of administrative agencies which resemble court proceedings. The holding of court–like hearings which end in decisions called ''orders.''

QUASI-LEGISLATIVE. Actions of administrative agencies which resemble legislative acts. The issuance of rules by an agency.

QUID PRO QUO. That which is given in return for something else, something for something. In contract law it constitutes legal consideration.

QUIS CUSTODIE IPSOS CUSTODES. Latin for who will regulate the regulators.

QUORUM. The number of members in an organization or body required to conduct business. Often a quorum is set at a majority of the entire membership.

QUO WARRANTO, WRIT OF. An action to establish that a company or official no longer holds a franchise or office because of failure to function or of misconduct.

RATIO DECIDENDI. Latin for the ''reason for the decision.'' The very essence or central core of a judicial opinion, the principle of the case. To find the ratio decidendi it must be established which facts are treated by the judge as material and immaterial.

REAL PROPERTY. Ownership of land.

REASONABLE DOUBT. See "Proof beyond a reasonable doubt."

RECOMMENDED DECISION. The decision of an administrative law judge. It is subject to the agency decision to accept it.

RECORD. The complete history, i.e., the written formal account of a case in either a lower court or an administrative agency. Its importance centers upon the detailed description which is then the basis of review by an appellate court. Particularly pertinent to administrative law, an agency should establish a "paper trail" regarding any order issued. This is necessary for purposes of review.

RECUSATION. Because of possible prejudice a judge is disqualified from hearing a case. May be requested through motion of litigants or may be voluntary.

REMAND. To send back. A reviewing court will send a case back to an agency or lower court; i.e., remand it for action in conformity with the principles decided by the reviewing court.

REMEDY. The legal means through a court order to enforce a right or to redress or compensate for a harm.

RESIDUUM RULE. See "Legal residuum rule."

RES JUDICATA. Sometimes res a judicata. Latin for "a thing decided." It is a fundamental principle in civil proceedings that once a conflict has been decided by the court, the decision is conclusive and the parties may not bring the same case before the court again.

RES NOVA. Latin for "a new thing" or matter. Refers to a new legal question which has not been decided before.

RESPONDEAT SUPERIOR. Latin maxim for the principle that when an agent or employee incurs a liability in carrying out a duty imposed by his employer, the employer bears responsibility.

RESPONDENT. The party to a lawsuit against whom a petition is brought. Also called an appellee.

RESTITUTION. To restore or to make good on something. For example, to return or pay for a stolen item.

RIGHT. The legal ability to perform or refrain from performing actions, or the ability to control objects in one's possession. It also entails the ability to control the actions of others. In a legal sense a right is enforceable by law as distinguished from a moral right.

RIPENESS. Courts will decline to review a case until it has developed, i.e. ripened, into a legal controversy to the point where it is entirely ready for appraisal by the regular courts. Cf. Exhaustion, Primary jurisdiction.

RULE-MAKING ON THE RECORD. The process of rule-making that follows the adjudicative process designated by section 554 of the federal Administrative Procedure Act and described in sections 556 & 557.

RULE-MAKING PROCEDURE. Agency process for promulgating rules, as contrasted with orders. Most critics suggest that whenever possible rule-making is preferable. It is set forth in § 553 of the federal Administrative Procedure Act.

RULES. When an agency acts in its legislative capacity to establish a norm, it is called a rule. Cf. Orders.

RULES OF EVIDENCE. In Anglo-American law, those rules developed for court cases decided by a jury, and proscribing what sorts of testimony or proof, i.e. evidence, may be presented legally in a case. There is a question about whether these rules have any reasonable application to agency litigation.

SCIENTER. With knowledge; prior knowledge that the act was wrong.

SCINTILLA. A particle, the least bit. Usually refers to the least particle of evidence in a case.

SCOPE OF REVIEW. When review of agency action by a court is legitimate it may include pertinent legal and constitutional questions and the meaning of terms, and it may compel action or set aside agency action on appropriate designated grounds.

SELF-EXECUTING. Legislative enactments, judicial decisions, agreements, or documents requiring no further official action to be implemented.

SERIATIM. Latin for individually, one by one, in order, point by point. The practice of judges' writing and recording their own views of a case. This practice is opposed to a collective opinion of the court representing the views of the majority, minority, or the whole court. Before the accession of John Marshall to the U.S. Supreme Court, the seriatim practice was generally employed in that court.

SHOW CAUSE ORDER. A command to a person to appear in court to explain why the court should not take a proposed course of action or accept a point of law before it.

SOVEREIGN IMMUNITY. Certain areas are said to be fully within the authority of the administration and are not subject to court review. A usual example is foreign relations. In domestic law it usually refers to the inability to sue government for money damages without its consent.

STANDING TO SUE. Sometimes referred to as simply, standing. The necessity of a plaintiff to demonstrate that he has a personal and vital interest in the outcome of the legal case or controversy brought before the court.

STARE DECISIS. Latin for "let the decision stand," abide by or adhere to decided cases. A deeply rooted common law tradition that once a court has determined a legal principle for a given set of facts, all future cases with similar facts should be decided in the same way.

STATUTE. A law enacted by a legislative body.

STATUTE OF LIMITATIONS. A legislative enactment prescribing a limited time period within which a legal suit may be started for a given offense or action.

SUA SPONTE. Latin phrase indicating that an action has been taken by a court on its own volition, i.e. without a motion to that effect by either party.

SUBPOENA. An order from a court or other duly authorized body to appear and testify before it.

SUBPOENA AD TESTIFICANDUM. A subpoena by which a witness is ordered to appear and testify in court.

SUBPOENA DUCES TECUM. A subpoena by which a witness is ordered to appear in court to testify and to bring and produce all pertinent documents.

SUB SILENTIO. Latin phrase to indicate an opinion that arrives at a result different from the apparent controlling case without specifically overruling it. It is said to have overruled the latter "silently" in such a case.

SUBSTANTIAL EVIDENCE. The standard of evidence usually required of agencies. Though less than a "preponderance of evidence" it is "more than a mere scintilla," i.e., "such relevant evidence as a reasonable mind might accept as adequate to support a conclusion." Accordingly, in reviewing an agency action a court will often determine only that a finding is indeed supported by evidence. In so doing it need not weigh the evidence, but only determine that there is a rational basis in the record for the finding. Cf. Proof beyond a reasonable doubt; Preponderence of evidence.

SUBSTANTIVE LAW. The basic law governing relationships; e.g., criminal law, constitutional law, property law, family law, torts. Substantive law is to be contrasted with procedural law; e.g., law of evidence.

SUMMARY JUDGMENT. Disposal of a case by a court or an agency prior to the completion of the full trial.

SUMMARY PROCEEDING. Any judicial business conducted that is disposed of before a court in a quick and simplified manner, sometimes without a jury or indictment. For the U.S. Supreme Court it entails a judgment without the benefit of oral arguments.

SUMMONS. A legal notice to a named defendant that he or she is being sued and must appear in court at a given time and place.

SUNSHINE LAWS. Laws which require that records, rules, findings, opinions, decisions, orders, and other data be open to the public. See § 552 of Administrative Procedure Act.

TEST CASE. A lawsuit brought to clarify, overturn, or establish a legal principle. It is usually sponsored by an interest group, but nevertheless there is a bona fide litigant.

TORT. A civil wrong or injury inflicted upon another. It does not include contract matters. Examples include negligence, defamation of character, and wrongful death. Government is usually able to avoid such responsibility, often expressed by the adage "the king can do no wrong". However, with restrictions, government usually permits some damage suits by passing tort claim acts.

TRANSCRIPT OF RECORD. It is a printed record of the proceedings of a court case or of an administrative hearing. It is used by an appellate court in reviewing the proceedings.

TREATY. A formal agreement between or among sovereign states creating rights and obligations under international law. In the U.S. all treaties must be ratified by a two-thirds vote of the Senate.

TRIAL DE NOVO. *See* De novo.

ULTRA VIRES. Latin, meaning outside or beyond authority or power. A term indicating an action taken outside the legal authority of the person or body performing it.

UNREVIEWABLE ORDERS. Courts will probably not review agency actions in matters where the statutory authority seeks to exempt agency action from review. The courts will also avoid review where ripeness, standing and exhaustion of remedies are incomplete.

VENUE. The location within a jurisdiction where a legal dispute is tried by a court.

VIRES. Latin for powers, force, (plural of vis). *See* Ultra vires.

WAIVER. The voluntary surrender of a legally enforceable right, privilege, or benefit. For example, when a criminal defendant gives up the right to remain silent by taking the witness stand on his own behalf.

WARRANT. A legal instrument issued by a judicial magistrate to arrest someone or to search premises.

WRIT. An order, in the form of a letter, from a court commanding that something be done.

WRIT OF CERTIORARI. *See* Certiorari, writ of.

WRIT OF ERROR. *See* Error, writ of.

WRIT OF MANDAMUS. *See* Mandamus, writ of.

WRIT OF QUO WARRANTO. *See* Quo warranto, writ of.

7

Selected Bibliography

This chapter is a selected, undifferentiated bibliography which includes both works devoted to administrative law and works on public administration which include pertinent sections and also some foreign language–English law dictionaries. It is arranged alphabetically. U.S. government reports are included under "U.S."

Most of the listings are in English but a few sources in foreign languages are also included.

Abrams, Norman. *Administrative Process: Alternatives to the Criminal Process.* Washington: The National Center for Administrative Justice, 1979.

Alibert, Raphael. *Le contrôle juridictionel de l'administration au moyen du recours pour excès de pouvoir.* Paris: Payot, 1926.

Allen, Carleton Kemp. *Bureaucracy Triumphant.* London: Oxford University Press, 1931.

American Enterprise Institute for Public Policy Research. *Government Regulations: Proposals for Procedural Reform.* Washington: American Enterprise Institute for Public Policy Research, 1979.

American Enterprise Institute for Public Policy Research. *Regulatory Reform: A Survey of Proposals in the 94th Congress.* Washington: American Enterprise Institute, 1976.

Anderson, Stanley V. *Canadian Ombudsman Proposals.* Berkeley: Institute of Governmental Studies, University of California, 1966.

Anderson, Stanley V. *Ombudsman Papers: American Experience and Proposals.* Berkeley: Institute of Governmental Studies, University of California, 1969.

Anderson, Ralph J. B. *Anglo-Scandinavian Law Dictionary.* Oslo: Universitetsforlaget, 1977.

Argis, Chris, et al. *Regulating Business: The Search for an Optimum.* San Francisco: Institute for Contemporary Studies, 1978.

Asimov, Michael R. *Administrative Law.* 8th ed. Gardena, Calif.: Gilbert Law Summaries, 1981.

Asimov, Michael. *Advice to the Public from Federal Administrative Agencies.* New York: M. Bender, 1973.

Attorney General's Committee on Administrative Procedure. *Administrative Procedure in Government Agencies.* (S. Doc #8, 77th Cong., 1st sess.). Washington: U.S. Government Printing Office, 1941.

Attorney General's Committee on Administrative Procedure. *Administrative Procedure in Government Agencies.* (S. Doc. #10, 77th Cong., 1st sess.). Washington: U.S. Government Printing Office, 1941.

Aucoc, Leon. *Conferences sur l'administration et le droit administratif.* 3rd ed. 3 vols. Paris: Dunod, 1882–86.

Auerbach, Carl A., Garrison, Lloyd K., Hurst, Willard, and Mermin, Samuel. *The Legal Process; An Introduction to Decision-making by Judicial, Legislative, Executive, and Administration Agencies.* San Francisco: Chandler Publishing Co., 1961.

Ball, Howard. *No Pledge of Privacy: The Watergate Tapes Litigation.* Port Washington, N.Y.: Kennikat Press, 1977.

Baram, Michael S. *Alternatives to Regulation.* Lexington: Lexington Books, 1982.

Barry, Donald D. and Whitcomb, Howard R. *The Legal Foundations of Public Administration.* St. Paul: West Publishing Co., 1981.

Bates, William N. *Administrative Codes and Registers: 1981 State/Federal Survey.* National Association of Secretaries of State, Administrative Codes and Registers Committee. Nashville: ACR Committee, [1981].

Beer, Henry Ward. *Federal Trade Law and Practice.* Chicago: Callaghan, 1942.

Belonzi, Arthur; D'Antonio, Arthur; Helford, Gary, and Associates. *The Weary Watchdogs: Governmental Regulators in the Political Process.* Wayne, N.J.: Avery Publishing Group, 1977.

Bender, Bernd. *Allgemeines Verwaltungsrecht.* Freiburg: Verlag Eberhard Albert, 1956.

Benjamin, Robert M. *Administrative Adjudication in the State of New York.* [No publisher, or place of publication], 1942.

Bennett, Marion T. *The United States Court of Claims: A History Part I: The Judges 1855-1976.* Washington: Superintendent of Documents, 1976.

Berkley, George E. *The Craft of Public Administration.* 3rd ed. Boston: Allyn and Bacon, Inc. 1981.

Bernard, Paul. *La notion d'ordre public en droit administrativ.* Paris: Librarie generale de droit et de jurisprudence, 1962.

Berthelemy, H. *Traite elementaire de droit administratif.* 13th ed. Paris: Rousseau, 1933.

Beseler-Jacobs, V. *Law Dictionary.* (German-English) New York & Berlin: Walter De Gruyter, 1971.

Beiber, Doris M. *Dictionary of Legal Abbreviations Used in American Law Books.* Buffalo: William S. Hein & Co., 1979.

Bienenfeld, Solomon. *Michigan Administrative Law.* Ann Arbor: The Institute of Continuing Legal Education, 1978.

Bishop, Joseph W. Jr. *Justice Under Fire: A Study of Military Law.* New York: Charterhouse, 1974.

Blackly, Frederick F. and Oatman, Miriam E. *Federal Regulatory Action and Control.* Washington: Brookings Institution, 1940.

Blair, Roger D. and Stephen Ruben. *Regulating the Professions.* Lexington, Mass.: Lexington Books, 1980.

Bonnard, Roger. *Le Controle juridictionnel de l'administration: etude de droit administratif compare*. Paris: Librairie Delagrave, 1934.

Bonnard, Roger. *Precis de droit administratif*. 4th ed. Paris: Librairie generale de droit et de jurisprudence, 1943.

Bradfute, Richard Wells. *The Court of Private Land Claims: The Adjudication of Spanish and Mexican Land Grant Titles, 1891-1904*. Albuquerque: University of New Mexico Press, 1975.

Brecht, Arnold. *The Art and Technique of Administration in German Ministries*. Cambridge: Harvard University Press, 1940.

Breyer, Stephen G. and Stewart, Richard B. *Administrative Law and Regulatory Policy*. Boston: Little, Brown and Co., 1979.

Brigham, John, and Brown, Don W., eds. *Policy Implementation: Penalties or Incentives*. New York: Law & Business, 1981.

Brown, L. Neville; Garner, J. F. and Questiaux, Nicole. *French Administrative Law*. London: Butterworths, 1967.

Brown, Michael K. *Working the Street: Police Discretion and the Dilemmas of Reform*. New York: Russell Sage Foundation, 1981.

Brown, Peter G. *Personal Liability of Public Officials, Sovereign Immunity, and Compensation for Loss*. Columbus, Ohio: Academy for Contemporary Problems, 1977.

Burrus, Bernie R. *Administrative Law and Local Government*. Ann Arbor: University of Michigan Law School, 1963.

Caiden, Gerald E., ed. *The Ombudsman: An International Handbook*. Westport, Conn.: Greenwood Press, 1982.

Carr, Cecil Thomas. *Concerning English Administrative Law*. New York: Columbia University Press, 1941.

Carrow, Milton M. *The Background of Administrative Law*. Newark, N.J.: Associated Lawyers Publishing Co., 1940.

Cary, William L. *Politics and the Regulatory Agencies*. New York: McGraw Hill, 1967.

Chamberlain, Joseph P.; Dowling, Noel T. and Hays, Paul R. *The Judicial Function in Federal Administrative Agencies*. Freeport, N.Y.: Books for Libraries Press, 1970 (reprint).

Clagett, Helen C. *Administration of Justice in Latin America*. New York: Oceana Publications, 1952.

Clarkson, Kenneth W. and Murris, Timothy J., eds. *The Federal Trade Commission Since 1970: Economic Regulation and Bureaucratic Behavior*. New York: Cambridge University Press, 1981.

Cofer, M. Donna Price. *Administering Public Assistance: A Constitutional and Administrative Perspective*. Port Washington, N.Y.: Kennikat Press, 1982.

Coleman, James K. *State Administration in South Carolina*. New York: Columbia University Press, 1935.

Comer, John Preston. *Legislative Functions of National Administrative Authorities*. New York: Columbia University Press, 1927.

Cooper, Frank E. *Administrative Agencies and the Courts*. Ann Arbor: University of Michigan Law School, 1951.

Cooper, Frank E. *State Administrative Law*. 2 vols. Indianapolis: The Bobbs-Merrill Co., 1965.

Cooper, Phillip. *Public Law and Public Administration*. Palo Alto, Calif.: Mayfield Publishing Co., 1982.

Cortner, Richard C. *The Bureaucracy in Court: Commentaries and Case Studies in Administrative Law*. Port Washington, N.Y.: Kennikat Press, 1982.

Council of Europe. *The Protection of the Individual in Relation to Acts of Administrative Authorities: An Analytical Survey of the Rights of the Individual in the Administrative Procedure and His Remedies against Administrative Acts*. Strassbourg: Council of Europe, 1975.

Courtney, Phoebe. *The Federal Monster*. Littleton, Colo.: Independent American Newspaper, 1976.

Cowen, Wilson, Nichols, Philip Jr., and Bennett, Marion T. *The United States Court of Claims: A History Part II: Origin—Development—Jurisdiction 1855-1978*. Washington: U.S. Superintendent of Documents, 1978.

Cushman, Robert E. *The Independent Regulatory Commissions*. New York: Oxford University Press, 1941 (Reprinted by N.Y.: Octagon Books, 1972).

David, Shirley H. *Researching Administrative Law*. St. Paul: Hamline University School of Law, (no date).

Davison, Forrester J. and Grundstein, Nathan D. *Cases and Readings on Administrative Law*. Indianapolis: Bobbs-Merrill, 1952 (Greenwood reprint, 1979).

Davis, Kenneth Culp. *Administrative Law and Government*. 2d ed. St. Paul: West Publishing Co., 1975.

Davis, Kenneth Culp. *Administrative Law Text*. 3rd ed. St. Paul: West Publishing Co., 1972.

Davis, Kenneth Culp. *Administrative Law Treatise*. 2d ed., 3 vols. San Diego, Calif.: K. C. Davis Publishing Co., 1978, 1979, 1980.

Davis, Kenneth Culp. *Discretionary Justice, A Preliminary Inquiry*. Baton Rouge: Louisiana State University Press, 1969.

Davis, Kenneth Culp, & European Associates. *Discretionary Justice in Europe and America*. Urbana: University of Illinois Press, 1976.

Davis, Kenneth Culp. *Police Discretion*. St. Paul: West Publishing Co., 1975.

DeSmith, S. A. *Constitutional and Administrative Law*. 2d ed. London: Penguin, 1973.

DeSmith, S. A. and Evans, J. M. *DeSmith's Judicial Review of Administrative Action*. 4th ed. London: Stevens & Sons, 1980.

Dicey, A. V. *Introduction to the Study of the Law of the Constitution*. 10th ed. by E. C. S. Wade. London: Macmillan, 1959.

Dickenson, John. *Administrative Justice and the Supremacy of Law in the United States*. New York: Russell & Russell, Inc., 1927.

Diez, Manuel Maria. *Derecho Administrativo*. Tomo I. Buenos Aires: Bibliografica Omeba, 1963.

Dimock, Marshall E. *Law and Dynamic Administration*. New York: Praeger, 1980.

Dimock, Marshall Edward; Dimock, Gladys Ogden, and Koenig, Louis W. *Public Administration*. Rev. ed. New York: Rinehart & Co., Inc., 1960.

Dubroff, Harold. *The United States Tax Court: An Historical Analysis*. Chicago: Commerce Clearing House, Inc., 1979.

Ducrocq, Theophile G. A. *Cours de droit administratif et de legislation francais* 7th ed. Paris: A. Fontemainf, 1897–1905.

Duez, Paul. *Les Actes de Gouvernement*. Paris: Sirey, 1935.

Duez, Paul. *La responsabilite de la puissance publique*. 2nd ed. Paris: Dalloz, 1938.

Duez, Paul et Guy Debeyre. *Traite de droit administratif*. Paris: Dalloz, 1952.

Duguit, Leon. *Law in the Modern State*. New York: B. W. Huebsch, 1919.

Dussault, Rene. *Le Controle Judiciare de l'administration au Quebec*. Quebec: Les presses de l'Universite-Laval, 1969.

Edles, Gary J. and Nelson, Jerome. *Federal Regulatory Process: Agency Practices & Procedures*. New York: Law & Business, 1981.

Egbert, Lawrence Deems, Fernando Morales-Macedo. *Multilingual Law Dictionary* (English, Francais, Espanol, Deutsch). Dobbs Ferry, N.Y.: Oceana Publications/Sijthoff/Nomos Verlagsgesellschaft, 1978.

Elcock, H. J. *Administrative Justice*. London: Longman's, Green, and Co., Ltd., 1969.

Etzioni-Halevy, Eva. *Political Manipulation and Administrative Power: A Comparative Study*. Boston: Routledge, 1980.

Everett, Robinson O. *Military Justice in the Armed Forces of the United States*. Harrisburg, Pa.: Military Service Publishing Co., 1956 (Reprinted by Greenwood Press, 1976).

Fain, Tyrus G., editor & compiler with collaboration of Katherine C. Plant, Ross Millary. *Federal Reorganization: The Executive Branch*. Public Document Services. New York: R. R. Bowker, 1977.

Farmer, J. A. *Tribunals and Government*. London: Weindenfeld and Nicolson, 1974.

Farrington, Robert Leslie. *The Limitations Upon the Delegation of Power by the Federal Legislature*. Washington: The Catholic University of America Press, 1941.

Fazal, M. A. *Judicial Control of Administrative Action in India and Pakistan*. Oxford: Clarendon Press, 1969.

Feist, Hans-Joachim. *Die Entstehung des Verwaltungsrechts als Rechtsdisziplin*. Munchen: Verlag UNI-Druck, 1968.

Fesler, James W. *Area and Administration*. University: University of Alabama Press, 1949.

Fins, Harry George. *Illinois Administrative Procedure*. Chicago: Current Law Publishing Co., 1942.

Florida Administrative Practice. 2d ed. Tallahassee: Cont. Legal Ed. Florida, 1981.

Foulkes, David. *Introduction to Administrative Law*. London: Butterworths, 1964.

Fox, Harrison W. *How to do Business in Washington: A Manager's Handbook of Governmental Relations*. New York: Collier-Macmillan, 1981.

Frank, Jerome. *If Men Were Angels: Some Aspects of Government in a Democracy*. New York: Harper & Bros., 1930.

Frankfurter, Felix, J. and Davison, Forrester, ed. *Cases and Other Materials on Administrative Law*. New York: Commerce Clearing House, 1932.

Freedman, James O. *Crisis and Legitimacy: The Administrative Process & American Government*. Cambridge [Eng.], New York: Cambridge University Press, 1978.

Freedman, James O. *The Administrative Process and American Government*. New York: Cambridge University Press, 1978.

Freedom of Information Act and Amendments of 1974 (P.L. 93-502) Source Book: Legislative History, Texts, and other Documents. Washington: U.S. Government Printing Office, 1975.

Freedom of Information Act Source Book: Legislative Materials, Cases, Articles. Washington: U.S. Government Printing Office, 1974.

Freund, Ernst. *Administrative Powers Over Persons and Property: A Comparative Survey*. Chicago: University of Chicago Press, 1928.

Freund, Ernst. *Cases on Administrative Law Selected From Decisions of English and American Courts*. St. Paul: West Publishing Co., 1911.

Freund, Ernst; Fletcher, Robert V.; Davies, Joseph E.; Pound, Cuthbert W.; Kurtz, John A; and Nagel, Charles. *The Growth of American Administrative Law*. St. Louis: Thomas Law Book Company, 1923.

Friendly, Henry J. *The Federal Administrative Agencies: The Need for Better Definition of Standards*. Cambridge: Harvard University Press, 1962.

Fritschler, A. Lee. *Smoking and Politics*. 3rd ed. Englewood Cliffs: Prentice Hall, 1983.

Frost, Anne and Howard, Carol. *Representation and Administrative Tribunals*. London: Routledge & Kegan Paul, 1977.

Galeotti, Sergio. *The Judicial Control of Public Authorities in England and Italy*. London: Stevens and Sons, Ltd., 1954.

Ganz, G. *Administrative Procedure*. London: Sweet and Maxwell, 1974.

Gardner, Jack L., ed. *The Book of the States 1982-1983*. Vol. 34. Lexington, Ky.: The Council of State Governments, 1982.

Garner, John F. *Administrative Law*. London: Butterworths, 1963.

Gellhorn, Ernest, and Boyer, Barry B. *Administrative Law and Process in a Nutshell*. St. Paul: West Publishing Co., 1981.

Gellhorn, Walter; Byse, Clark; and Strauss, Peter L. *Administrative Law Cases and Comments*. 7th ed. Mineola, N.Y.: The Foundation Press, 1979.

Gellhorn, Walter. *Ombudsmen and Others: Citizen's Protectors in Nine Countries*. Cambridge: Harvard University Press, 1966.

Gellhorn, Walter. *Federal Administrative Proceedings*. Baltimore: Johns Hopkins Press, 1941 (Greenwood reprint, 1972).

Gellhorn, Walter. *When Americans Complain: Governmental Grievance Procedures*. Cambridge: Harvard University Press, 1966.

Ghauja, B. R. *Law and Procedure of Departmental Inquiries (in Private and Public Sectors . . .)*. 2d ed. Lucknow (India): Eastern Book Co., 1981.

Goodnow, Frank J. *Comparative Administrative Law*, two volumes in one. New York: G. P. Putnam's Sons, 1893.

Goodnow, Frank J. *The Principles of the Administrative Law of the United States*. New York: G. P. Putnam's Sons, 1905.

Gordon, Richard S. *Issues in Health Care Regulation*. New York: McGraw-Hill, 1980.

Government Regulation: Proposals for Procedural Reform 1979, 96th Congress, 1st Session. Washington: American Enterprise Institute, 1979.

Green, Mark J., ed. *The Monopoly Makers: Ralph Nader's Study Group Report on Regulation and Competition*. New York: Grossman, 1973.

Griffith, J.A.G. and Street, H. *Principles of Administrative Law*, 2d ed. London: Sir Isaac Pitman & Sons, Ltd., 1957.

Griffith, J.A.G., ed. *From Policy to Administration: Essays in Honor of William A. Robson*. London: George Allen & Unwin, 1976.

Haines, Charles G. and Dimock, Marshall E., eds. *Essays on the Law and Practice of Governmental Administration: A Volume in Honor of Frank Johnson Goodnow*. Baltimore: Johns Hopkins Press, 1935. (Greenwood reprint, 1968.)

Hamline University, School of Law. *Minnesota Practice Methods: Minnesota Administrative Practice*. St. Paul: Hamline University, 1981.

Hardy, Paul T. and Weeks, J. Devereux. *Personal Liability of Public Officials Under Federal Law*. Athens, Ga.: Institute of Government, University of Georgia, 1981.

Hart, James. *An Introduction to Administrative Law with Selected Cases*. 2nd ed. New York: Appleton-Century Crofts, Inc., 1950.

Hartley, T. C. *Foundations of European Community Law: An Introduction to the Constitutional and Administrative Law of the European Community*. New York: Oxford, 1981.

Hassumani, A. P. *Some Problems of Administrative Law in India*. New York: Asia Publishing House, [c. 1964].

Hauriou, Maurice. *La jurisprudence administrative de 1892 a 1929*. 3 vols. Paris: Sirey, 1929.

Hauriou, Maurice. *Precis de droit administrativ et de droit public*. 12th ed. Paris: Sirey, 1933.

Havinghurst, Clark C., ed. *Administrative Discretion*. Dobbs Ferry, N.Y.: Oceana Publications, Inc., 1974.

Hayek, Friedrich A. *The Constitution of Liberty*. Chicago: University of Chicago Press, 1960.

Healy, Robert E., ed. *Federal Regulatory Directory 1979–80*. Washington: Congressional Quarterly, Inc., 1979.

Henderson, Edith G. *Foundations of English Administrative Law.* Cambridge: Harvard University Press, 1963.

Herring, E. Pendleton. *Federal Commissioners: A Study of Their Careers and Qualifications.* Cambridge: Harvard University Press, 1936.

Hewart, The Rt. Hon. Lord [Gordon]. *The New Despotism.* London: Ernest Benn Limited, 1929.

Hill, Myron G., Jr.; Rossen, Howard M.; and Sogg, Wilton S. *Administrative Law for Law School and Bar Examinations.* 2d ed. (Smith's Review Legal Gem Series). St. Paul: West, 1977.

Holland, Charleton III.; Kemp, Kindra; and staff, eds. *Representing Clients Before and Against Administrative Agencies.* Berkeley: California Continuing Education of the Bar, 1977.

Holoch, Alan and Mubarak, Jill. *Comparative Constitutional and Administrative Law.* Los Angeles: University of Southern California Law Center, 1979.

Horowitz, Donald L. *The Courts and Social Policy.* Washington: Brookings Institution, 1977.

Hurwitz, Leon. *The State as Defendant: Governmental Accountability and the Redress of Individual Grievances.* Westport, Conn.: Greenwood Press, 1981.

Hucker, Charles O. *The Censorial System of Ming China.* Stanford: Stanford University Press, 1966.

Hudson, Manley O. *International Tribunals: Past and Future.* New York: Carnegie Endowment for International Peace, 1944.

Illinois House Democratic Staff. *Administrative Rules and Regulations.* Springfield: Illinois General Assembly, House Executive Committee, 1976.

Iluyomade, B. O. and Eka, B. U. *Cases and Materials on Administrative Law in Nigeria.* Ile-Ife, Nigeria: University Ife Press, 1980.

Issalys, Pierre, (for Law Reform Commission of Canada). *The Pension Appeals Board: A Study of Administrative Procedures in Social Security Matters.* Ottawa: Law Reform Commission of Canada, 1979.

Jackson, Paul. *Natural Justice.* 2d ed. London: Sweet and Maxwell, 1979.

Jaffe, Louis L. and Nathanson, Nathaniel L. *Administrative Law: Cases and Materials.* 4th ed. Boston: Little, Brown and Co., 1976.

Jaffe, Louis L. *Judicial Control of Administrative Action.* Boston: Little, Brown and Co., 1965.

Jain, M. P. *Administrative Law of Malaysia and Singapore.* Singapore: Malayan Law Journal, 1980.

Jain, S. N. and Jain, M. P. *Principles of Administrative Law.* 3rd ed. Bombay: Tripathi, 1979.

Jenks, C. Wilfred. *The Proper Law of International Organizations.* London: Stevens & Sons Ltd., and Dobbs Ferry, N.Y.: Oceana Publications, 1962.

Jeze, Gaston P. A. *Principes generaux du droit administratif.* 3rd ed. 6 vols. Paris: M. Giard, 1925–36.

Joint Committee on Continuing Legal Education of the Virginia State Bar. *Virginia Administrative Law & Practice*. Charlottesville: Virginia State Bar & Virginia Bar Assn., 1980.

Jowell, Jeffrey L. *Law and Bureaucracy: Administrative Discretion and the Limits of Legal Action*. Port Washington, N.Y.: Dwellen Publishing Co., Inc., and Kennikat Press Corp., 1975.

Kagan, Robert A. *Regulatory Justice: Implementing a Wage-Price Freeze*. New York: Russell Sage Foundation, 1978.

Kalodner, Howard I. and Fishman, James J., eds. *Limits of Justice: The Courts' Role in School Desegregation*. Cambridge: Ballinger Publishing Co., 1978.

Kammholz, Theophil C. and Strauss, Stanley R. *Practice and Procedure Before the National Labor Relations Board*. 3rd ed. Philadelphia: ALI/ABA, 1980.

Kaplan, Neil A.; Friedman, Paul L.; Bennett, Robert S.; and Trainor, Helen C. *Parallel Grand Jury and Administrative Agency Investigations*. Chicago: American Bar Association/Professional Education Publications, 1981.

Kavanagh, John A. *A Guide to Judicial Review*. Toronto: Carswell Co., Ltd., 1978.

Kerse, C. S. *EEC Antitrust Procedure*. London: European Law Center, 1981.

Kessler, Marie-Christine. *Le Conseil d'etat*. Paris: Armand Colin, 1968.

Kim, Joe T. *New Readings in Public Administration*. Dubuque, Iowa: Kendall, 1980.

Koh, Byung Chul. *The United Nations Administrative Tribunal*. Baton Rouge: Louisiana State University Press, 1966.

Kohlmeier, Louis M., Jr. *The Regulators*. New York: Harper and Row, 1969.

Kohlmeier, Louis M., Jr. *Watchdog Agencies and the Public Interest: The Regulators*. New York: Harper and Row, 1969.

Kraines, Oscar. *The World and Ideas of Ernst Freund: The Search for General Principles of Legislation and Administrative Law*. University: University of Alabama Press, 1974.

Kramer, Fred A. *Dynamics of Public Bureaucracy: An Introduction to Public Management*. 2d ed. Cambridge: Winthrop Publishers, 1981.

Laferriere, Edouard L. J. *Traite de la juridiction administrative et des recours contentieux*. 2d ed. 2 vols. Paris: Berger-Levrault, 1896.

Landis, James M. *The Administrative Process*. New Haven: Yale University Press, 1938. Greenwood Press reprint, 1974.

Landis, James M. *Report on Regulatory Agencies to the President-Elect*. Reprint by Pike and Fisher, Administrative Law, 1960.

Laubadère, André de. *Traité de droit administratif*. 8th ed. 2 vols. Paris: Librairie generale de droit et de jurisprudence, 1980.

Law Commission. *Working Paper No. 40: Remedies in Administrative Law*. London: H. Majesty's Stationery Office, 1973.

Law Reform Commission of Canada. *Independent Administrative Agencies*. Ottawa and Montreal: Law Reform Commission of Canada, 1980.

Law Society of Upper Canada. *Administrative Practice and Procedure*. Toronto: R. de Bero, 1971.

Legislative Reference Service of the Library of Congress. *Separation of Powers and the Independent Agencies: Cases and Selected Readings*. S. Doc. #91–49. 91st Cong., 1st sess. Washington: U.S. Government Printing Office, 1970.

Leive, David M. *International Regulatory Regimes*. 2 vols. Lexington, Mass: Lexington Books, D. C. Heath, 1976.

Linde, Hans A. and Bunn, George. *Legislative and Administrative Processes*. Mineola, N.Y.: The Foundation Press, Inc., 1976.

Lipscomb, Abner E. *Judicial Control of Administrative Action in Texas*. Waco: Baylor University Press, 1938.

Long, Kathleen D. "Sources and Materials in California Administrative Law." M.L.S. Thesis, University of California, Los Angeles, 1976.

Lorch, Robert S. *Democratic Process and Administrative Law*. Detroit: Wayne State University Press, 1969.

Lorch, Robert S. *Public Administration*. St. Paul: West Publishing Co., 1978.

Lowenberg, Bernward. *Die Geltendmachung Von Geldforderungen im Verwaltungsrecht*. Berlin: Duncker & Humblot, 1967.

Lutrin, Carl E. and Settle, Allen K. *American Public Administration: Concepts and Cases*. 2d ed. Palo Alto, Calif.: Mayfield Publishing Co., 1980.

MacAvory, Paul W. *The Crisis of the Regulatory Commissions: An Introduction to a Current Issue of Public Policy*. New York: W. W. Norton & Co., 1970.

Manheim, Jarol B. *American Politics Yearbook, 1982–83*. New York: Longman, 1982.

Marx, Fritz Morstein, ed. *Elements of Public Administration*. New York: Prentice Hall, 1946.

Mashaw, Jerry L. and Merrill, Richard A. *Introduction to the American Public Law System: Cases and Materials*. St. Paul: West Publishing Co., 1975.

Massey, I. P. *Administrative Law*. Lucknow (India): Eastern Book Co., 1980.

Matthews, Elizabeth W. *Access Points to the Law Library Card Catalog Interpretation*. Buffalo, N.Y.: Wm. S. Hein Co., 1982.

Mayers, Lewis. *The American Legal System: The Administration of Justice in the United States by Judicial, Administrative, Military and Arbitral Tribunals*. New York: Harper & Bros., 1955.

McDowell, Douglas S.; Huhn, K. C.; & Assoc. *NLRB Remedies for Unfair Labor Practices*. Philadelphia: University of Pennsylvania, Wharton School, 1976.

McFarland, Carl. *Judicial Control of the Federal Trade Commission and the Interstate Commerce Commission 1920–1930: A Comparative Study of the Relations of Courts to Administrative Commissions*. Cambridge: Harvard University Press, 1933. (Johnson Corp. reprint, 1968).

McFarland, Carl and Vanderbilt, Arthur T. *Cases and Materials on Administrative Laws*. 2d ed. Albany: Bender, 1952.

Mezines, Basil J.; Stein, Jacob A. and Gruff, Jules. *Administrative Law*. 6 vols. New York: Matthew Bender, 1981.

Michael, James R., with Ruth C. Fort, eds. for Ralph Nader's Center for Study of Responsive Law. *Working on the System: A Comprehensive Manual for Citizen Access to Federal Agencies*. New York: Basic Books, 1974.

Miewald, Robert D. *Public Administration: A Critical Perspective*. New York: McGraw Hill, 1978.

Miller, Edward B. *Administrative Appraisal of the NLRB*. 3rd ed. Philadelphia: Wharton School, 1981.

Miller, J. Bennett. *An Outline of Administrative and Local Government Law in Scotland*. Edinburgh: W. Green and Sons Ltd., 1961.

Miller, William T., and Monaco, Grace Powers. *Outline of Administrative Law*. Irvington-on-Hudson, N.Y.: Blackstone Law Summaries, 1975.

Millett, John D. *Government and Public Administration: The Quest for Responsible Performance*. New York: McGraw-Hill Book Co., 1959.

Misra, Anand Swarup. *Commentaries on U.P.* [Uttar Pradesh:] *Public Services (Tribunals) Act*, 2d ed. Lucknow, India: Eastern Book Co., 1980.

Mitnick, Barry M. *The Political Economy of Regulation*. New York: Columbia University Press, 1980.

Morgan, Glenn G. *Soviet Administrative Legality*. Stanford: Stanford University Press, 1962.

Murphy, Patrick J., ed. *Rules and Regulations: A Compilation of 50 State Administrative Procedures Acts*. Arlington, Va.: Federal-State Reports, Inc., 1979.

Musolf, Lloyd D. *Federal Examiners and the Conflict of Law and Administration*. Baltimore: Johns Hopkins Press, 1953.

National Association of Attorneys General. *Official Liability: Immunity Under Section 1983*. Raleigh, N.C.: Committee on the Office of the Attorney General, 1979.

Neumann, Mary M., ed. *Washington Information Directory 1981–82*. Washington: Congressional Quarterly, Inc., 1981.

Nigro, Felix A., and Nigro, Lloyd G. *Modern Public Administration*. 5th ed. New York: Harper & Row, 1980.

Noll, Roger G. *Reforming Regulation: An Evaluation of the Ash Council Proposals*. Washington: Brookings Institution, 1971.

Nonet, Philippe. *Administrative Justice: Advocacy and Change in a Government Agency*. New York: Russell Sage Foundation, 1969.

Owen, Bruce M. and Braeutigam, Ronald. *The Regulatory Game: Strategic Use of the Administrative Process*. Cambridge: Ballinger Publishing Co., 1978.

Parish, David W. *State Government Reference Publications: An Annotated Bibliography*. 2d ed. Littleton, Colo. Libraries Unlimited, Inc., 1981.

Parker, Reginald. *Administrative Law: A Text*. Indianapolis: Bobbs-Merrill Co., 1952.

Patterson, Edwin W. *The Insurance Commissioner in the United States: A Study in Administrative Law and Practice*. Cambridge: Harvard University Press, 1927.

Paulsen, Monrad G., ed. *Legal Institutions Today and Tomorrow*. New York: Columbia University Press, 1959.

Pennock, Rolland J. *Administration and the Rule of Law*. New York: Farrar and Rinehart, 1941.

Pfiffner, John M. and Presthus, Robert. *Public Administration*. 5th ed. New York: Ronald Press, 1967.

Phillips, Almarin, ed. *Promoting Competition in Regulated Markets*. Washington: Brookings Institution, 1970.

Phillips, O. Hood. *Constitutional and Administrative Law*. 4th ed. London: Sweet and Maxwell, 1967.

Ponder, Lester M. *United States Tax Court Practice and Procedure*. Englewood Cliffs: Prentice Hall, 1976.

Pound, Roscoe. *Administrative Law: Its Growth, Procedure and Significance*. Littleton, Colo.: Fred B. Rothman & Co., 1981. (Originally University of Pittsburgh, 1942).

Pound, Roscoe. *The Spirit of the Common Law*. Francistown, N.H.: Marshall Jones Co., 1921.

Quemner, Thomas A. *Dictionnaire Juridique Francais-Anglais*. Paris: Editions de Navarre, 1976.

Quirk, Paul J. *Industry Influence in Federal Regulatory Agencies*. Princeton, N.J.: Princeton University Press, 1981.

Ramasubramaniam, K. A. *Commissions of Inquiry Act*. Bombay: Tripathi, 1980.

Redford, Emmette S. *Democracy in the Administrative State*. New York: Oxford University Press, 1969.

Redlich, Norman. *The Law of Urban Affairs: Cases, Problems, Materials*. 2 vols. New York: New York University School of Law, 1968.

A Reference Manual to Accompany Understanding the Federal Regulatory Process: And How to Improve Your Access To It. Washington: Washington Monitor, Inc., 1980.

Rendel, Margherita. *The Administrative Functions of the French Conseil d'Etat*. London: London School of Economics and Political Science, 1970.

Rhyne, Charles S.; Rhyne, William S.; and Elmendorf, Stephen P. *Tort Liability and Immunity of Municipal Officials*. Washington: National Institute of Municipal Law Offices, 1976.

Rich, Giles S. *A Brief History of the United States Court of Customs and Patent Appeals*. Washington: [Superintendent of Documents], 1980.

Richardson, Ivan L., and Baldwin, Sidney. *Public Administration: Government in Action*. Columbus, Ohio: Charles E. Merrill Publishing Co., 1976.

Rideout, Roger. *Industrial Tribunal Law*. London & New York: McGraw-Hill, 1980.

Robb, Louis A. *Dictionary of Legal Terms: Spanish English and English Spanish*. New York: John Wiley & Sons, 1955.

Robinson, Glen O. and Gellhorn, Ernest. *The Administrative Process*. St. Paul: West Publishing Co., 1974.

Robson, William A. *Justice and Administrative Law: A Study of the British Constitution*. 3rd ed. London: Stevens & Sons, 1951, (Greenwood reprint, 1970.)

Rocky Mountain Mineral Law Foundation. *Natural Resources Administrative Law and Procedure*. Boulder, Colo.: 1981.

Romain, Alfred. *Dictionary of Legal and Commercial Terms*. (English-German) Vol. I. Munchen: C. H. Beck'sche Verlogsbuckhandlung, 1975. (German-English), Vol. II, 1980.

Rowat, Donald Cameron, ed. *The Ombudsman, Citizen's Defender* 2d ed. London: Allen & Unwin, 1968.

Rowat, Donald C., ed. *Administrative Secrecy in Developed Countries*. New York: Columbia University Press, 1979.

Ruhlen, Merritt. *Manual for Administrative Law Judges*. Washington: Government Printing Office, 1974.

Sackman, Julius, L. *Nichols' the Law of Eminent Domain*. Revised 3rd ed. 10 vols. New York: Matthew Bender, 1981.

Schechter, A. H. *Interpretation of Ambiguous Documents by International Administrative Tribunals*. New York: Praeger, 1964.

Schwartz, Bernard. *Administrative Law*. Boston: Little, Brown and Co., 1976.

Schwartz, Bernard. *Administrative Law: A Casebook*. Boston: Little, Brown and Co., 1977.

Schwartz, Bernard and Wade, H. W. R. *Legal Control of Government: Administrative Law in Britain and the United States*. Oxford: Clarendon Press, 1972.

Schwartz, Bernard, ed. *The Economic Regulation of Business and Industry*. 5 vols. New York: Chelsea House & R. R. Bowker, 1973.

Schwartz, Bernard. *French Administrative Law and the Common-Law World*. New York: New York University Press, 1954.

Schwartz, Bernard. *An Introduction to American Administrative Law*. 2d ed. Dobbs Ferry, N.Y.: Oceana, 1962.

Schwartz, Bernard. *The Professor and the Commissions*. New York: Alfred A. Knopf, 1959.

Seabra, Fagundes, M. *O controle dos atos administrativos pelo poder judiciaro*. 3rd ed. Rio de Janeiro: Revista Forense, 1957.

Serra Rojas, Andres. *Derecho Administrativo*. Mexico, D. F.: Libreria de Manuel Parrua, 1961.

Shapiro, Martin. *The Supreme Court and Administrative Agencies*. New York: The Free Press, 1968.

Sharfman, Robert J., ed. *Administrative Law*. Springfield: Illinois Institute for Continuing Legal Education, 1976.

Sharfman, I. L. *The Interstate Commerce Commission; A Study in Administrative Law and Procedure*. 4 vols. New York: Commonwealth Fund, 1931-37.

Sherrill, Robert. *Military Justice is to Justice as Military Music is to Music*. New York: Harper & Row, 1970.

Simmons, Robert H., and Dvorin, Eugene P. *Public Administration: Values, Policy, and Change*. New York: Alfred Publishing Co., 1977.

Smith, Gordon B. *The Soviet Procuracy and the Supervision of Administration.* Alphan an den Rijn: Sijthoff & Noardhoff, 1978.

Sothe, S. P. *Administrative Law.* 3rd ed. Bombay: Tripathi, 1979.

Stason, E. Blythe. *The Law of Administrative Tribunals,* 2d ed. Chicago: Callaghan & Co., 1947.

Stephens, Harold M. *Administrative Tribunals and the Rules of Evidence.* Cambridge: Harvard University Press, 1933.

Swenson, Rinehart John. *Federal Administrative Law.* New York: Ronald Press, 1952.

Sullivan, Linda E., ed. *Encyclopedia of Governmental Advisory Organizations.* 3rd ed. Detroit: Gale Research Co., 1980.

Takwani, C. K. *Lectures on Administrative Law.* Lucknow (India): Eastern Book Co., 1979.

Taylor, Hannis. *Due Process of Law and Equal Protection of the Laws.* Chicago: Callaghan & Co., 1917.

Tomain, Joseph P. *Energy in a Nutshell.* St. Paul: West Publishing Co., 1981.

Rucker, Edwin W. *Text-Cases-Problems on Administrative Law, Regulation of Enterprise, and Individual Liberties.* St. Paul: West Publishing Co., 1975.

Uhler, Armin. *Review of Administrative Acts; A Comparative Study of the Doctrine of the Separation of Powers and Judicial Review in France and the United States.* Ann Arbor: University of Michigan Press, 1942.

University of British Columbia, Faculty of Law. "Proceedings of the Administrative Law Conference." 18–19 October, 1979. Vancouver, B.C.: University of British Columbia, 1979.

U.S. Commission on Organization of the Executive Branch of the Government. *Task Force Report on Regulatory Commissions.* [Appendix N] Washington: U.S. Government Printing Office, 1949.

U.S. Commission on Organization of the Executive Branch of the Government. *Task Force Report on Legal Services and Procedure.* Washington: U.S. Government Printing Office, 1955.

[U.S.] Comptroller General of the U.S. *Management Improvements in the Administrative Law Process.* . . [A Report]. Washington: General Accounting Office, 1979.

U.S. Congress. House. Report by the subcommittee on Oversight and Investigations of the Committee on Interstate and Foreign Commerce. *Federal Regulations and Regulatory Reform.* [Govt. Classification # Y4. In 8/4:R26/8]. 94th Cong., 2d sess., 1976.

U.S. Congress. Senate. Committee on the Judiciary. *Administrative Procedure Act: Legislative History.* S. Doc. 248. 79th Cong., 2nd sess., 1946.

U.S. Court of Military Appeals. *Military Law and Military Justice.* [Washington]: Librarian, U.S. Court of Appeals, 1972.

U.S. Department of Defense. *Manual for Courts-Martial United States.* Rev. ed. Washington: U.S. Government Printing Office, 1969.

U.S. Department of Justice. *Attorney General's Manual on Administrative Procedure Act.* 1947; (reprint): Holmes Beach, Fla.: W. W. Gaunt, 1973.

U.S. Department of Justice. *Attorney General's Memorandum on the 1974 Amendments to the Freedom of Information Act.* Washington: U.S. Government Printing Office, 1975.

U.S. Department of Justice. *Attorney General's Memorandum on the Public Information Section of the Administrative Procedure Act.* Washington: U.S. Government Printing Office, 1967.

U.S. Office of the Federal Register. *The Federal Register: What it is and How to Use it.* . . Washington: Office of the Federal Register, 1977.

[U.S.] President's Advisory Council on Government Organization. *A New Regulatory Framework: Report on Selected Independent Regulatory Agencies.* Washington: U.S. Government Printing Office, 1971.

[U.S.] President's Committee on Administrative Management. *Report of the Committee with Studies of Administrative Management in the Federal Government.* Washington: U.S. Government Printing Office, 1937.

Van Vleck, William C. *The Administrative Control of Aliens; A Study in Administrative Law and Procedure.* New York: Commonwealth Fund, 1932.

Vandervart, Linda. *Political Control of Independent Administrative Agencies.* Ottawa & Montreal: Law Reform Commission of Canada, 1979.

Vasan, R. S., ed. *Latin Words and Phrases for Lawyers.* Ontario: Law and Business Publications (Canada) Inc., 1980.

Vedel, Georges. *Droit administrativ.* 2d ed. Paris: Presses Universitaires de France, 1961.

Vocino, Thomas and Rabin, Jack. *Contemporary Public Administration.* New York: Harcourt Brace Jovanovich, Inc., 1981.

Wade, Henry William Rawson. *Towards Administrative Justice.* Ann Arbor: University of Michigan Press, 1963.

Wade, H. W. R. *Administrative Law.* 5th ed. Oxford: Clarendon Press, 1982.

Waldo, Dwight. *The Study of Public Administration.* Garden City, N.Y.: Random House, 1955.

Waline, Marcel. *Manuel elementaire de droit administratif.* 4th ed. Paris: Recueil Sirey, 1946.

Warren, George, ed. *The Federal Administrative Procedure Act and the Administrative Agencies.* New York: NY University School of Law, 1947.

Warren, Kenneth F. *Administrative Law in the American Political System.* St. Paul: West Publishing Co., 1982.

Weil, Prosper. *Le droit administratif.* 2d ed. Paris: Presses Universitaires de France, 1966.

Welborn, David M. *Governance of Federal Regulatory Agencies.* Knoxville: University of Tennessee Press, 1977.

Wheare, K. C. *Maladministration and Its Remedies.* London: Stevens & Sons, 1973.

White, Anthony G. *Administrative Adjudication, the Hearing Officer/Administrative Judge: A Selected Bibliography.* Monticello, Ill.: Vance Bibliographies, 1980.

White, Leonard D. *Introduction to the Study of Public Administration*. 4th ed. New York: Macmillin, 1955.

Whitmore, H. *Principles of Australian Administrative Law*. Sydney: Law Book, 1980.

Whyatt, John. *The Citizen and the Administration: The Redress of Grievances*. London: Stevens, 1961.

Williams, David G. *Maladministration: Remedies for Injustice: A Guide to the Powers and Practice of the British Ombudsmen and Similar Bodies*. London: Oyez Pub., 1976.

Willis, John. *The Parliamentary Powers of English Government Departments*. Cambridge: Harvard University Press, 1933.

Willoughby, W. W. and Fenwick, C. G. *Types of Restricted Sovereignty and of Colonial Autonomy*. Washington: Government Printing Office, 1919.

Wilson, Geoffrey. *Cases and Materials on Constitutional and Administrative Law*. 2d ed. Cambridge: Cambridge University Press, 1976.

Wilson, James Q. *The Politics of Regulation*. New York: Basic Books, 1980.

Woll, Peter. *Administrative Law: The Informal Process*. Berkeley: University of California Press, 1963.

Woll, Peter, ed. *Public Administration and Policy: Selected Essays*. New York: Harper Torchbooks, 1966.

Wright, Nancy D.; and Allen, Gene P.; Herner and Co., comp. *The National Directory of State Agencies 1980-81*. Arlington, Va.: Information Resources Press, 1980.

Yeager, Dennis R. *Representing Government Officials in Litigation 1981*. New York: Practicing Law Institute, 1981.

Zanobini, Guido. *Corso di diritto amministrativo*. 6th ed. 6 vols. Milano: A Giuffre, 1942-1959.

INDEX

Acts Cited by Popular Name, 42
Administrative codes, 35, 36–37
Administrative decisions, 23–29
  Am. Jur. 2d, 38
  looseleaf publications, 30–31
  official reports, 24–28
  Shepards citations, 50
Administrative discretion
  informal actions, 9
  literature on, 70–71
Administrative law judge, 7, 9, 23
Administrative lawmaking, 3, 4, 5
Administrative procedure
  literature on, 62
  national and state laws, 1
  rules and regulations, 33–35,
    36–37, 42; See also, rule-making
Administrative Procedure Act, 1, 4, 5, 6, 7,
    8, 9, 23, 41, 51, 52
Administrative registers, 36–37
Advance Sheets (Lawyers' Edition), 19
Advisory opinions, 10
Agency investigation, 38
A.L.A. Schechter Poultry Copp. v. United
    States, 48–49
Allen, Carleton Kemp, 67
Allen, Gene P., 65, 66
American Association of Law Libraries, 54,
    55
American Bar Association, 52
American Digest System, 44–47
American Enterprise Institute, 52
American Jurisprudence 2d (Am. Jur. 2d),
    35, 38–39, 40, 42, 47, 93
American Law Reports (A.L.R.), 21–22, 39,
    93
American Political Science Review, 96
Anderson, Stanley V., 66
Annotations, 19, 21–22, 38, 42, 43
Argyris, Chris, 68
Asimov, Michael R., 76
Atlantic Reporter, 32

Attorneys general opinions, 10
AUTO-CITE, 56
Baldwin, Sidney, 77
Bankruptcy Reporter (West), 32
Barry, Donald D., 61
Bates, William N., 65
Bender Bernd, 74
Benjamin, Robert M., 66
Bennett, Marion T., 71
Berkley, George E., 77
Bias and interest, 7
Bibliography, 80–82; See also Footnoting
    and Bibliography
Big seven, 68
Bishop, Joseph W. Jr., 72
Blue book, See Harvard, and State
Book review indexes, 54, 55
Boyer, Barry B., 76
Bradfute, Richard Wells, 71
Brief
  definition and purpose of, 11–13
  elements of, 13–15
  model of, 15–16
Briefs of counsel, 11, 19
Brown, L. Neville, 73
Brown, Michael K., 70
Bunn, George, 61
Burden of proof
  administrative hearings, 8–9
Bureau of National Affairs (BNA), 23
Burris, Bernie R., 66
Byse, Clark, 61
Calder v. Bull, 19
California Reporter, 29
Case-method, 12
Century Digest, 44
Chicago Manual of Style, 81
Circuit courts of appeal, 20
Citators, 47, 48–52; See also Shepards
Clagett, Helen C., 75
Clarkson, Kenneth W., 68
Class brief, See brief

Clear and convincing evidence
  rule, 7
Codes
  Administrative, 35, 36–37
    Code of Federal Regulations (C.F.R.),
      33, 34, 35, 93
  Shepard's, 52
  State, 41, 94
  United States, 41–43, 94
Comer, John Preston, 67
Commerce Clearing House (CCH), 23
Commerce Court of the U.S., 21
Common law, 12, 18
Comparative administrative law, 2, 55
  literature on, 72–75
Computer assisted research, 56
Concurring opinions, 15
Confidentiality, personal records, 4
Connected case, 51
Cooper, Frank E., 62, 66
Cooper, Phillip, 61
Corpus Juris Secundum (C.J.S), 35, 38
    39–41, 46, 93
Court cases (footnotes), 92–93; See also
    Legal citations
Court of International Trade, 21
Court reporter, 19, 21
Court reports, 18–23, 29, 32
Cowen, Wilson, 71
Cumulative supplements, 41, 43, 51
Current Law Index, 54–55
Cushman, Robert E., 70
Data acquisition
  agency activity, 1
Davis, Kenneth Culp, 61, 62, 70
Decennial Digest, 45
Deciding officer, 9
Delegated legislation, 35
Delegation of legislative authority, 1–2, 48,
    49
Descriptive-Word Index
  American Digest, 45
Dicey, A.V., 67
Dickerson, John, 67
Dicta, 14
Dictionaries, 56–57
Digests, 38, 43–47
  Descriptive-Word Index, 45, 46, 47
  regional, 56, 10n
  specialized, 46–47
  Table of Cases indexes, 45, 46, 47
Dimock, Gladys Ogden, 77

Dimock, Marshall Edward, 77
Discovery, 7
Discretion, See Administrative discretion
Discursive comments, 96; See also Ex-
    planatory footnotes
Dissenting opinions, 15
Dissertation
  footnoting and bibliography of 88, 98
Dubroff, Harold, 71
Duguit, Leon, 75
Dussault, Rene, 73
Dvorin, Eugene P., 77
Eight Decennial Digest, 44
Eka, B.U., 73
Eldon L. Smith (case name), 50
Elrod v. Burns, 45
Encyclopedias, 35–41, 86, 93
Estoppel, 2
Everett, Robinson O., 72
Evidence, 7
Exclusiveness of the record, 8
Executive privilege, 4
Exhaustion of remedies, 3
Ex parte communication, 8
Explanatory footnotes, 80, 92, 96
Facts, when to cite, 80
Facts on file, 53
Fazal, M.A., 73
Federal agency decisions, 23–29, 30–31
  footnote form, 94
  looseleaf publications, 23, 30–31
  official reports, 24–28
Federal Cases (F.Cas.), 20, 92
Federal Code Annotated, (F.C.A.), 42, 51
Federal court opinions, 20–21
Federal Digest, 46
Federal Register (Fed. Reg.), 5, 33–34, 35,
    43, 93
Federal Reporter (F.), 21, 93
Federal Rules Decisions (F.R.D.), 21, 93
Federal Rules of Civil and Criminal Pro-
    cedure, 21
Federal Practice Digest, 2d, 46
Federal statute
  footnoting of, 94
Federal Supplement (F. Supp.), 21, 93
Feist, Hans-Joachim, 73
Findings
  administrative hearings, 9
First Decennial Digest, 44
Footnotes
  form, 81, 82

general rules, 81–82
what to, 79–80
Footnoting and Bibliography of books
article in, 85
association as author, 85, 98
author, single (one), 82
author, more than one, 83, 97
author's name not on title page, 85
citation in one book from another book, 84
chapter in book, 85
edition other than first, 83
editor, 83
introduction or foreword to book by another author, 85
multivolume work, 84
paperback edition of book first published in hardcover, 84
series, 83, 84
series, one author, several volumes, different titles, 84
translator, 84
Footnoting and Bibliography of court cases, 18, 20, 21, 32, 92–93, 98
Footnoting and Bibliography in encyclopedias
conventional, 86
legal, 39, 41, 93
Footnoting and Bibliography of government documents
Congressional
bills, 89
debates, 89
hearings, 89
reports, 89
Executive
from an executive department, 89–90
presidential papers, 90
International
international organization, 90
treaties, 91
State and local, 91
Footnoting and bibliography of journal articles,
legal journals, 55, 95, 98
nonlegal, 85–86, 98
Footnoting and bibliography of legal materials, 92–96, 97, 98
Footnoting and bibliography of magazine articles, 86
Footnoting and bibliography of newspapers, 86

Footnoting second or later references, 95–96
Freedom of Information Act, 4
Fritschler, Lee A., 68
Galeotti, Sergio, 75
Gardner, Jack L., 65
Garner, J.F., 73
Gellhorn, Ernest, 76
Gellhorn, Walter, 61, 69, 74, 76
General Digest, 44, 45
General indexes
research tools, 38, 40, 41, 42, 43, 53, 54, 55
General Orders in Bankruptcy (Shepard's), 51
Goodnow, Frank J., 67, 75
Government information sources
literature on, 64–65
Government Organization Manual, 64, 88
Gruff, Jules, 61
Guide to Periodical Literature, 53
Hart, James, 62
Harvard Blue Book, 92
Havinghurst, Clark C., 70
Hayek, Friedrich A., 67
Headnotes, 19, 20
Healy, Robert E., 65
Hearings
administrative, 7
congressional, 89
institutional decisions, 8, 9
officer (hearing), 7
Hearsay evidence, 7
Hewart, Gordon, 67
Hill, Myron G. Jr., 76
Historically significant literature, 66–68
Holoch, Alan, 73
Hucker, Charles O., 74
Hudson, Manley O., 76
Hybrid rule-making, 4, 5
H.W. Wilson Company, 53
Ibid., 95
Illinois Administrative Procedure Act, 6, 8
Illinois Bar Association, 52
Iluyomade, B.O., 73
Index to Foreign Legal Periodicals, 55
Index to Legal Periodicals, 53, 55
Index to Periodical Articles Related to Law, 53, 55
Informal actions and discretion, 9
Informal rule-making, 4
Informational Access Corporation, 54

Institute of Advanced Legal Studies of the
    University of London, 55
Institutional decisions, 8, 9
International Administrative law
    literature on, 75–76
International law, 55
Interpretative notes, 43
Interpretative rule-making, 5
Interviews
    footnotes and bibliography, 87
Jaffe, Louis L., 61, 69
James-Chapman Index to Legal Periodicals,
    53
Jenks, C. Wilfred, 76
Jowell, Jeffrey L., 70
Judicial notice, 8
Judicial review, 1, 2–3
Key Number System, 32, 44–46
Koenig, Louis W., 77
Koh, Byung Chul, 76
Kramer, Fred A., 77
Landis, James M., 69
Laubadère, Andfe de, 73
Law review (journal) articles
    administrative law journals, 52–53
    code references, found in, 42
    indexes for, 52–55
    U.S.C.S., feature of, 43
Lawyers Co-operative Publishing Company
    and the Bancroft-Whitney Com-
    pany, 19, 20, 21, 39, 42, 46, 56
Legal Citators, See Citators
Legal encyclopedias, 35–41, 93, 94
Legal periodicals, See law review
Legislative courts
    literature on, 71–72
Legislative histories, 41, 42
Legislative rule-making, 5
Leive, David M., 75
Letters
    footnoting and bibliography, 87
LEXIS, 56
Linde, Hans A., 61
List of Subject Headings
    Index to Legal Periodicals, 54
Lorch, Robert S., 77
LSA: List of CFR Sections Affected, 34
Lutrin, Carl E., 77
Manheim, Jarol B., 64
Manual for Writers of Term Papers, Theses
    and Dissertations, 81
Manuscript collections
    footnoting and bibliography, 87

Marx, Fritz Morstein, 78
Matthew Bender and Company (MB), 23
Matthews, Elizabeth W., 35
McGraw Hill, 47
Mead Data Central, 56
Menzines, Basil J., 61
Michael, James R., 68
Miewald, Robert D., 77
Military justice
    literature on, 72
Military Justice Reporter, 29
Miller, J. Bennett, 74
Miller, William T., 76
Millett, John D., 78
Mimeographed reports
    footnoting and bibliography, 87
Model State Administrative Procedure Act,
    23
Modern Federal Practice Digest, 46
Monaco, Grace Powers, 76
Morgan, Glenn G., 74
Mubarak, Jill, 73
Murris, Timothy J., 68
Musolf, Lloyd D., 69
Nathanson, Nathaniel L., 61
National Association of Secretaries of State,
    35, 65
National digest, 44
National Reporter System, 20, 29, 44
Neumann, Mary M., 64
New York Court of Appeals, 29
New York Supplement, 29
Nichols, Philip Jr., 71
Nigro, Felix A., 77
Nigro, Lloyd G., 77
Ninth Decennial, 44
Nonprinted reports
    footnoting and bibliography, 87
North Eastern Reporter, 32
North Western Reporter, 32
Obiter dicta, 14
Official notice, 8
Official reports and studies
    literature on, 62–64
Ombudsman, 2, 10, 55
Outline series, literature on, 76
Pacific Reporter, 32
Pamphlets
    footnoting and bibliography, 87
Panama Refining Co., v. Ryan, 33
Paper read or speech delivered
    footnoting and bibliography, 88
Parallel citations, 13, 18, 48, 49

Parish, David W., 65
Peanut butter case, 5
Pfiffner, John M., 77
Pike and Fisher Administrative Law Service, 29, 44
Pleadings
   pretrial agency process, 7
Pocket supplement, 39, 43, 46
Ponder, Lester M., 71
Popular Names and Tables, 41–42
Pound, Roscoe, 67
Predictability
   agency decisions, 6
Preponderance of evidence, 7
Presthus, Robert, 77
Pretrial process, 7
Primary jurisdiction, 3
Procedural rules, 5, 29, 38, 42, 44
Proceedings of a Meeting or Conference
   footnoting and bibliography, 88
Public Administration texts
   literature pertaining to law, 76–78
Quasi-judicial function, 1, 5, 6, 12
Quasi-legislative function, 1
Questiaux, Nicole, 73
Quotations, 79–80
Rabin, Jack, 77
Radio and Television
   footnoting and bibliography, 87
Reasonable doubt, 7
Redlich, Norman, 66
Regional and state digests, 44
Registers, 36–37
Regulatory agencies
   literature on, 68–70
Rendel, Margherita, 73
Rich, Giles S., 71
Richardson, Ivan L., 77
Ripeness, 3
Robson, William A., 75
Rojas, Andres Serra, 74
Rowat, Donald C., 74
Rule-making, 1, 4–5, 6, 38
Sage Public Administration Abstracts, 53
Sage Publications, 96
Schechter, A. H., 76
Schwartz, Bernard, 52, 61, 68, 69, 73, 74
Scientific Reference form, 96–98
Scope-notes, 47
Securities and Exchange Commission v. Chenery, 18
Separation of functions, 8
Separation of powers, 67

Settle, Allen K., 77
Shapiro, Martin, 69
Shepardizing, *See* Citators
Shepard's Acts and Cases by Popular Name, 47, 51
Shepard's Citations, Inc., 47, 48
Shepard's Code of Federal Regulations Citations, 47, 52
Shepard's United States Citations: Cases, 47, 48
Shepard's United States Administrative Citations, 47, 49–51
Shepard's United States Citations: Statutes, 47, 51–52
Sherrill, Robert, 72
Sick chicken case, 48–49
Simmons, Robert H., 77
Slip opinion, 19
South Eastern Reporter, 32
Southern Reporter, 32
South Western Reporter, 32
Sovereign immunity, 2
Standing, 3
Stare decisis, 6, 18, 41
Stason, E. Blythe, 62
State administrative law decisions
   looseleaf services, 33
State blue books, 64
State codes, 35, 36–37
State court cases, 29, 32, 93
State and local administrative law
   literature on, 65–66
State registers, 35, 36–37
Statutes at Large (U.S.), 42, 51
Statutory law, 38, 41, 42, 51
Stein, Jacob A., 61
Strauss, Peter L., 61
Subject and Author Index
   legal index, 54
Subpoena, 4
Substantial evidence rule, 7
Sub verbo, 86
Sullivan, Linda E., 65
Summary judgment, 7
Sunshine acts, 4, 42
Supreme Court (U.S.) opinions
   reported in, 18–20
Supreme Court Reporter (S.Ct.), 18, 20, 48
Syllabuses, 19
Table of Abbreviations, 39
Table of Cases Commented Upon, 54
Table of Cases Index, 45
Table of Statutes Commented Upon, 54

Temporary Emergency Court of Appeals, 21
Thesis
  footnoting and bibliography, 88, 98
Topic and Key Number, 45
Tort liability, 2
Treatises, major
  literature on, 61–62
Tucker, Edwin Wallace, 62
Turabian, Kate L., 81
Vocino, Thomas, 77
Voting coalition, 15
Wade, E.C.S., 67
Wade, H.W.R., 73
Warren, George, 70
Warren, Kenneth F., 60
Welborn, David M., 68
Whitcomb, Howard R., 61
White, Leonard D., 78
West digest system, 44
Western Political Quarterly, 96
WESTLAW, 56
West Publishing Company, 20, 21, 29, 40, 43, 44, 46, 47, 56
West reporter system, 23, *See also*, National Reporter System
West's Bankruptcy Reporter, 32
Woll, Peter, 69, 77
Word Index to U.S. Supreme Court Reports: Lawyers' Edition, 47

Wright, Nancy D., 65
Uniform State Laws, 38
Uniform Systems of Citation, 81, 92, 94–95
United Nations
  footnotes and bibliography, 91
United States Circuit Courts, 20, 21
United States Code (U.S.C.), 41–42, 51, 52
United States Code Annotated (U.S.C.A.), 41, 43, 51
United States Code Congressional and Administrative News, 43
United States Code Service (U.S.C.S.), 41, 42, 43, 47
United States Constitution, 42, 43, 51, 95
United States Court of Appeals, 21
United States Court of Custom and Patent Appeals, 21
United States District courts, 20, 21, 52
United States Government Manual, 64, 88
United States Statutes at Large, 42, 51
United States Supreme Court, 18–20, 46, 47, 48, 92
United States Supreme Court Reports—Lawyers' Edition (L.Ed.), 18, 19–20
United States Reports (U.S.), 18, 19, 48, 49, 92
United States Treaties and other International Agreements, 51